Advance Praise for Brave

Brave is well written, thoughtful, and important as an example of a personal journey through shyness. Helen Rivas-Rose shows how capitalizing on the strengths of shyness, and intelligently helping yourself to grow beyond painful, traumatic experiences in childhood, can lead to a powerfully meaningful and rich life. It is compelling to see how Helen began to recognize and build on her considerable talents, and then enjoy them. Shy people will benefit from reading this memoir. It helps to see that you are not alone.

Lynne Henderson, PhD,
Co-Director with Philip Zimbardo, PhD,
The Shyness Institute, Palo Alto, California

Helen Rivas-Rose has written a poignant memoir documenting her transition from painful, inhibiting chronic shyness to empowered self-confidence. *Brave* creates an honest portrait of a courageous woman who dared to face her suffering and overcome her self-consciousness to claim a fuller life. Many readers will resonate with her experience of loneliness and find inspiration in her determination at mid-life to take singing lessons and perform in concerts, to give talks, to run an art gallery, and subsequently to write her story. Tapping into her own inner strength, she learned to speak "from the heart" and to do so without fear. Her book is a moving testimony to her achievement.

Beth Darlington, PhD, board member,
C.G. Jung Institute of New York

ꙮ

I did not want this book to end. Helen-Rivas-Rose's story makes you feel that you can make a really important difference in your own life, and in that of another. Read this memoir with an open heart and you will learn about yourself. You may find yourself drawn to those who are held back by their fears of judgment, their feelings that they are different from others, their feelings of not fitting in. You may even find that those who at first seemed different are just like you and me.

Fredlee Ann Kaplan, LCSW, New York,
member, Chairman's Council of Gift of Life International

ꙮ

This book is a wonderful gift. Helen Rivas-Rose has given us a compelling account of her journey, in the midst of an eccentric and powerful family, traveling the world, all the while suffering with shyness. *Brave* persuades us to look deeper at shyness and its effects on children and adults alike. Readers who feel misunderstood or disconnected from this very social world will find inspiration through her story.

Julia Burns Riley, PhD, MSW

ꙮ

I could not put *Brave* down. The shyness theme is related as a disability in a delightfully fluid style that transcends the specific experience of the author. Probably everyone harbors an unfortunate personality trait that deserves introspection. Rivas-Rose's diligent studies and explorations over nearly six decades to find her cure, and thus bask in her lost passions in life, are truly inspirational.

Beverly Russell, author, educator,
San Miguel de Allende

ꝏ

Helen Rivas-Rose has written a Brave book! This intimate personal and family saga explores the life of a shy person who overcomes incredible obstacles to find her passion and live a fulfilling life. Her book can inspire others on their own journey out of shyness and into wholeness.

Mary MacQueen, PhD,
psychotherapist, Atlanta and Kennebunkport

ꝏ

Helen Rivas-Rose has won an enviable victory. Her book about overcoming shyness is a tribute to her focus and determination to change this aspect of her life. Read it for inspiration.

Dorcas H. Cofer, PhD,
clinical psychologist

BRAVE,

a Memoir of Overcoming Shyness

Helen Rivas-Rose

Helen Rivas-Rose

Periwinkle Publishing

BRAVE,

a Memoir of Overcoming Shyness

ISBN: 978-0-9827433-0-0

Periwinkle Publishing
1 Crescent Surf
Kennebunk, ME 04043
www.shynessbook.com

Design and layout by Nancy Grossman
Back Channel Press
www.backchannelpress.com

Printed in the United States of America

Library of Congress PCN 2010927421

Front Cover Photo: Mari Seder
Back Cover Photo: Diana Giardi

For shy people everywhere

and

to my children, Anthony and Conrad,

and

to my grandchildren, Noah and Simon

Long enough have you timidly waded, holding
a plank by the shore,
Now I will you to be a bold swimmer...

"Song of Myself"
—Walt Whitman

Contents

Prologue

It was a June day in 1964, and my turn. The president of the university called: "Helen Read Merrill, Bachelor's Degree in History." It was one of the worst moments of my life.

I didn't know that families participated in graduations, that my family should be in the audience watching me. Unable to form new friendships after my roommate left school at Christmas, I'd had no one to speak with about graduation, to learn what it entailed and I hadn't discussed it with my parents.

When I saw everybody else's family present, I imploded, a giant throbbing blob with tears trickling down my face as I struggled across the stage to receive my diploma. *What a horrible way to end university...alone. I'm forever alone. I can't make friends. For sure now I'll never be able to look back on my time in college and really love it, like Dad loves Williams. I'm done here now and have nothing to take from it. Mom and Dad are old and not in tune with my life. They let me do everything by myself.*

And the worst would happen. Shyness continued to block me from talking about myself and forming close friendships for another thirty years. How many times would I reproach myself with the same thought: *Nobody knows me simply because I can't speak up!*

Finally, in mid-life an event occurred that so shocked me I contacted a psychologist—a difficult step to take because I'd never dared talk to anyone about myself. It happened after my mother's death, when my brother Nat and I inherited several acres of land within an extended family compound in Kennebunk, Maine. Part of it was a beach at the end of a spit, a piece of land shaped like a finger surrounded by water on three sides. The cousins who owned the part connected to land built a road on it, and afterward said no one could use it without their permission.

I called one of these cousins to ask how Nat and I could reach our beach. Spitting words between her teeth, she replied, "You've no rights anywhere to the beach: YOU DON'T DESERVE ANY!"

I mumbled goodbye and ambled numbly to the end of my lane, wracking my brains. I couldn't understand how someone with whom I shared ancestry, someone with whom on occasion I sipped drinks, someone whose parent had participated in my mother's wedding, could be so callous. I now think she was afraid that Nat and I, with little money, might sell the beach lot, allowing strangers to live and drive near her house.

But on that afternoon, July 5, 1984, I felt I was a colossal, colossal failure in understanding people. Standing semi-paralyzed in the lane, I looked down and saw my pathetic lonely self at forty-one years of age and, after a moment, saw that self standing next to me at age eighty-two, white-haired and withered, still not knowing people. I vowed to confront my inability to get to know people: I would no longer muddle my mind with alcohol but instead find a psychologist to help me comprehend my fellow human beings.

Today I am not shy. But after that initial action of seeking help, it took nearly twenty-five years of effort to become totally healthy, to direct all my attention to who and what's before me, spending no energy dealing with shyness. I feel as liberated as a giant sea turtle, who, after being lost on land, reaches water. Although shyness is behind me, from time to time remnants of painful emotions associated with it surface, and I still hurt.

There should be no shame in being shy, but I used to feel very ashamed. Somehow, shyness doesn't afflict everyone; most people build barriers against it, like gardeners build fences to keep out critters. I didn't learn how to do this and remained unprotected and vulnerable to its stealthy, insidious attacks.

For decades, this trait skewed my decisions about every single significant choice I made–about my work, where I lived, whom I married and even how I raised my children. That demoralizing force cheated me of what could have been a more mature, productive and happy life. If only I'd sought professional help earlier!

Knowledge of and support for the severely shy is growing, but the problem is still not well understood. In 2005 I attended a New England wide conference on selective mutism, a term used to describe certain quiet children who speak normally at one location but hardly at all, or not at all, at others. I was one: until I was ten years old, I talked at home and at some relatives' homes, but almost no place else. Prior to the conference, I learned in an email with the director that I would be the only person attending who'd been a selective mute, that the other two hundred and fifty people present would be either parents or educators.

While showing slides in the darkened auditorium, the director asked the audience to describe characteristics of this type of shy child. They mentioned such things as being silent, having strange expressions on their faces at school, being happy at home and reluctant to leave it. My inner voice implored me over and over to tell everyone, "We're full of pain!"—but I was sobbing so hard I could not. That all those people gathered to help shy children overwhelmed me; how I wished they'd been there for me when I was small. Although I couldn't speak up about the hurt, during a break I wrote on a piece of paper, "Selective mutes are full of pain when they're alone, away from home"—and dropped it into the suggestion box.

Isolated

1

Cos Cob: Behind the Closed Door

I detested being locked in my bedroom. Since I can remember, from about three years of age until nine, my mother shut me up around six o'clock, or shortly after my father returned from work. Why? I presume it allowed her some needed peace to enjoy dinnertime with her husband. I remained in my room until the next morning.

From behind the fixed screen on my bedroom window, I searched the backyard to catch a glimpse of my parents and yell for attention. As the evening lengthened, I became more and more desperate and called "Mom, Mom!" louder and louder. My parents learned to stay out of sight, moving their Adirondack chairs so I couldn't see them and I would no longer bother to scream. Instead I stood by the window until I got exhausted from feeling lonely and then sat on my bed, waiting for my mother to see me.

After my parents had dinner, my mother would come upstairs and lie down on my bed with me until I slept, but her nearness didn't undo the discomforting feelings that had welled up while I was left alone, when all I could think of was,

I don't like being here. Everyone else is downstairs and I have to be here.

Other times my parents put me in my room as punishment for disobedience. I knew something was quite unjust: they locked me up when I was good, and they locked me up when I was bad. At those times I sobbed uncontrollably, and hollered, "I want to get out; I'll be good; let me out!" Though I cried out like that, they never once came to comfort me or let me out, not until long after I'd stopped crying, from fatigue.

When I was five, I accidentally cut myself on the soft fleshy part of my cheek, and, while locked in my room, I would pick it. One day my mother said, "Dr. Stringfield's coming today to put braces on your arms so you can't pick your sore. We have to let it heal so it won't leave a scar."

When he came, I sat on the edge of my bed, staring at my feet. He strapped boards onto my arms and taught my mother how to put them on and take them off.

The braces made me feel doubly helpless: I had the usual restraint of four walls but now could move only my legs! I felt extremely hurt that my parents concerned themselves over such a little cut, and yet did nothing to comfort me when I yelled, when I lost my breath from crying, when I felt empty and drained like no child should.

I disliked being kept in my room even more those evenings when relatives visited and everyone played music. My mother performed on the piano, my father the drums and cymbals, and a cousin the violin. Amid sounds of lively jazz and singing, I heard laughter. Leaning against my door, I told my stuffed dog Blackie, "I hate this."

My mother played the piano with all her being and undoubtedly it provided an escape valve for her emotions. She played classical, jazz and American popular music with equal gusto. One hot summer evening, when strands of Gershwin, Sousa and Chopin traveled through opened windows far out into the neighborhood, Guy Lombardo, on his way home to Stamford after a performance in New York City, stopped by to see who was playing. When years later my mother would tell me this story, her voice changed into an unfamiliar low pitch, exuding the pleasure this visit still meant to her.

But the story reminded me of the pain I associated with her lovely playing at parties and my being excluded from them. Being shut off from family in the evenings, together with having no children in the neighborhood left little opportunity to learn and practice the art of play.

ଊ

In addition to being caused by environmental factors, shyness, some psychologists believe, is partially inherited. I believe my mother, Helen Parsons Merrill, born in 1905, suffered more than a little from it. I know her father did. He gave away his second daughter at her wedding and then disappeared for the remainder of the day. Was my grandfather's shy disposition passed on to me through my mother?

Growing up, my mother spent much of her time with strict German nannies and black servants. "The nannies were terrible. They made us use rigid manners all the time," she told me, "but the black servants were oh-so-good natured and playful. They played with Anne, the twins and me (her siblings) with balls and lawn games, and I especially loved it when they hauled us around in small wagons. Sometimes they even hitched one of the goats to a cart and pulled us around."

My mother enjoyed reminiscing about this, yet oddly she seldom mentioned her parents except to say that every day, the nannies bathed and dressed them in clean clothing before "visiting" with them. From this it would seem she received little mothering from her own mother and thus didn't have a clear role model when she herself became a mother.

Each year my mother's family spent six months in Summerville, South Carolina, and the rest of the year in Kennebunk, Maine. The children grew up with a combination of home tutoring and two dissimilar school systems and cultures.

During high school my mother felt so miserable at her boarding school in Connecticut that she ran away. This sounds pretty brave to me. When I was a teenager, she used to describe her school life to me. "I couldn't do math; I couldn't understand it one bit, but the teachers kept after me to do it. And I hated the dances. I sat by myself all evening, and watched Anne (her sister who was two years younger) being asked to dance all the time. She was beautiful, and I was a tomboy."

After my mother quit school, she lived in New York City with a wealthy and sophisticated unmarried aunt, her father's oldest sister, Llewellyn. There she studied piano under one of New York City's best instructors, while attending lectures on floral arrangements, bird watching and bridge.

My father, Frederic Arnold Merrill, born in 1893 and nicknamed Ack, came from a background steeped in Unitarian philosophy and the attitudes of the now rare "proper" Bostonians. His father, Frederick Augustus Merrill, born in

1844, practiced dentistry on Beacon Hill. His clientele included Oliver Wendell Holmes, who had been his professor of anatomy at the Harvard School of Hygiene and Dentistry. My grandfather died in the 1913 flu epidemic and his wife twenty years later.

I have little reason to suspect my father suffered from shyness. I saw a list, written in his tiny slanted handwriting, of various club memberships, which suggested he led an active social life, first at Williams College, and, after he graduated and began work for the American Hawaiian Shipping Company in Los Angeles, at other social clubs.

In 1916 he attended a special six-month wartime program at the U.S. Naval Academy in Annapolis and graduated as a 1st Officers Class Reserve Ensign, U.S.N. One of six officers in command, my father spent eleven months nonstop in active duty (the longest on any wartime ship) onboard the destroyer USS *Cushing* in the Atlantic. After the war he worked for Standard Oil of New Jersey in New York City, where he eventually headed the shipping department.

In 1928, through an invitation from her sister Anne, my twenty-three-year-old mother attended a party where she met my thirty-seven-year-old father, a friend of Anne's fiancée. I have several amorous letters my father wrote my mother during their courtship, some expressing his desire to have children. Here's one.

> My Darling Helen,
>
> If ever a man was lonely, I am twice as lonely, I miss you so much. I just heard your wonderful voice over the telephone, it was great to have you reciprocate my good love

> greetings, I love you so much that my heart is almost ready to break......and oh how happy I shall be when we have some (children), I hope they are triplicates or more. You are so wonderful.... You are more than the whole world to me. We shall have to enjoy November every second for the next four months will be barren. I want to marry you now, sweetheart, and only convention stops it. You would marry me too, wouldn't you. I love you. I hope I do not die waiting. We can wait but it is terribly hard to.....
>
> All my love, Dearest, and happy dreams to you. I awake like an angel with you near me, oh it is so wonderful to picture you so.
>
> Good night, Your Ack, always.

None of my mother's letters to my father were saved. In April 1929, they married at Goose Creek Church in Summerville, South Carolina, and settled down in Forest Hills, in New York.

I heard little about the eleven-year period when my parents lived in New York except, during the 1938 hurricane, my father sailed his yacht out to sea, fearing waves would destroy it if moored. He was courageous to be alone at sea with huge waves and strong winds.

I also know, after eleven childless years, that my mother had an operation to be able to become pregnant. After conceiving, she enrolled in a child psychology course at Yale. With considerable pleasure she used to tell me, "I scored the highest of everyone in the class because I was so much more interested to learn about children than any of the other students in the class." I could never understand how someone who mastered a course on child psychology raised me the way she did, and to this day remain skeptical about some scholarly advice.

To shed light on her parenting, I tried to find the textbook she might have studied, but Yale officials said it was impossible to research so far back in the archives. I did learn that many child psychologists in the 1930s espoused rigid control, influenced by German educators. Some of them believed children had no personalities, that they were just little people going through a physical growing-up stage. Following this school of thought, did she think it wouldn't matter to lock me up every evening?

To raise their family, my parents gave up their suburban lifestyle and moved to a colonial home on seven acres with a pond, old stones walls and mature trees along the edge of the Mianus River in Cos Cob, Connecticut.

In 1940 few couples aged fifty and thirty-seven started families. Perhaps my parents didn't realize that childrearing could be so burdensome. I was born in 1942, two years after my only sibling Nathaniel, whom we called Nat.

ᘓ

I was named Helen, like my mother. Our facial features were similar: serious-looking blue eyes, light skin with rosy cheeks and angular chins. Though we both had light brown eyebrows, she had wavy, short brown hair, while my straight blond hair came down below my chin, and I needed a barrette to keep it out of my eyes. We were both thin, and she seemed especially tall. She usually wore a tailored suit with a tapered waist and a pretty blouse with a sparkling pin. Nat's facial features were similar to my mother's and mine, although his chin was a little squarer. He was well built and of average height.

My mother took care of Nat and me after my father left for work at six in the morning. I usually found her in the den, sitting in her pretty shiny black Hitchcock rocker with gold drawings stenciled along the top of the back. There she smoked cigarettes, read avidly, listened to classical music or stitched intricate crewelwork while I played with my toys on the floor. I loved it when she played the piano, which she did a couple of times a week. She was soft-spoken, which is what people generally say of me.

But because her voice was low, her presence around the house was not very strong, and sometimes I felt lost not knowing where she was. I never, ever heard her raise her voice or get angry, not even when I disobeyed her. I was, however, familiar with her facial expressions when she was worn out: her eyes slanted outwards, her jaw tightened and lines spread over her brow.

I have no memory of sitting in her lap or her hugging me, though she never forgot to kiss me goodnight. As a teenager, I felt agonized when I'd hear her say, "Educated people don't show their emotions by holding and hugging." How I'd wanted to be cuddled! Although my mother spent much of her time at home in order to be near her children, I didn't develop a warm relationship with her. It's possible this lack of bonding affected my attempts to make female friends both in school and in later life.

I don't know whether she had any close friends: I never saw her with one or heard her mention any. She talked a lot with Nana, her mother, both in person and on the phone. I would overhear them discuss plans to make certain chores easier for my mother, such as elevating the bathroom sink so she wouldn't have to bend over so much.

My baby book testifies that I knew early on my mother tired easily and also that I bore the brunt of it. My first complete sentence, at age one and a half, reads, "Mama tired—call Nana?" I only noticed this entry in 2005. Reading it produced a chilling thought: how many of my needs as a baby were not adequately met due to my mother's poor health?

When we visited towns, I wore a harness so Mama wouldn't have to run after me. I vaguely recall tugging on my leash when I went too far ahead. When I turned around and saw her in an A-line coat that came down to her calves, she appeared a giant. Although I was only two or three, I wondered why I was fastened to my mother—I saw other children moving around freely. I felt unlucky and uncomfortable.

I never learned the particulars of my mother's health while we lived in Cos Cob, though I observed she did little physical work, having a full-time cook and regular people to clean. She had poor circulation and rested a lot, thinking it would give her energy. Today we know the importance of exercise to develop energy, but back then people were less informed about health.

When I was fourteen, I discovered my mother suffered from weak mental strength as well. One day, not knowing I was within earshot, Nana made a reference to my mother about the summer she'd spent in a sanatorium. Shocked about my mother's problems, I tiptoed away, fearing for my own sanity.

I never mentioned this to anyone. I presume the reason for her stay in the institution was caused by depression and that Nana looked after Nat and me during her absence

2

With Others

As a toddler, when I tried to play with Nat, after a short time we usually began to argue. Then he would yell, "Mom, Helen's making a mess of my toys. She's bothering me. Make her leave." My mother's face would collapse into a frown as she carried me screaming to my room. Nat would crow, "Crybaby, crybaby, you're just a crybaby!" Many times, being the younger child, made me think I received unfair care.

We didn't always fight. I have a picture of us when I was seven and he nine fishing for freshwater crabs from a rock beside a river. That day he patiently taught me how to catch them while our mother waited for us on a nearby bridge.

As I grew older, we did fewer things together, even though I had no one else to play with. He had hobbies and interests that kept us apart. For example, my father made a baseball diamond for him; he collected mitts, bats and balls and played with friends, most of whom were a bit older, which meant several years older than I. Sometimes he talked to me about his activities, but I didn't have any to mention.

For two years my mother drove us several miles to Tiny Tots School, three times a week. During the 1940s, non-working mothers usually didn't take their children to preschool. I don't know whether she did it to give her some time away from us or for us to have children to play with. Maybe both.

I wanted to be able to fit in at Tiny Tots School, to play with the others, but I couldn't, even though I dreaded being by myself. I spent a lot of time standing alone under a tree with gigantic roots that snaked and twisted above the ground, waiting, waiting to go home.

From time to time, an adult would say, "Helen, come over here and play," but I didn't say anything or even look at her. Without moving, I kept my thoughts to myself. ***I don't know how; I don't know what to say.*** The teacher then said no more. Special care and treatment might have helped, but in those days, doctors taught parents and teachers to ignore shy behavior, saying it would go away by itself. Nothing could have done more harm: I needed counseling, in particular, help to learn how to talk and play.

☙

After we finished Tiny Tots, my mother enrolled Nat and me in Greenwich Country Day, a private school about five miles from home, where I excelled academically, receiving High Honors in all subjects. I didn't feel self-conscious when speaking directly to a teacher, although that seldom happened because in lower grades teachers didn't ask pupils many questions. I loved all the class assignments, but especially ones with numbers. While doing them I forgot about being ostracized on the playground, but as soon as the bell for recess rang, I fretted with anxiety.

The same discomfort plagued me in the dining room because I sat at a long table with a dozen other girls and had no idea how to talk with them. In addition to not having friends, there were foods I couldn't stand, and made me gag, such as watery, overcooked spinach. At home, while I was left alone to finish up, I hid the uneaten food under the table, on an expansion leaf, but at school I had to tuck what I could inside my paper napkin, furtively looking around to be sure no one was watching. I was always afraid the bulk or the moisture would disintegrate the napkin and expose my ploy.

I don't remember ever being caught at it, or being disciplined for anything at all, except in grade three, when a girl sitting behind asked me a question about our work.

I was so elated to have someone to talk with! When I finished my reply, in my enthusiasm, I said, "See?" I had merely wondered whether my explanation was sufficient or if she wanted more, but the teacher lambasted me in front of the class. "Helen! It's rude to say 'seeeee.' It shows you think you're too smart; don't ever, ever say that again." I was so embarrassed. But much, much worse, the girl never spoke to me again and I was too shy to say anything to her.

My great-aunt Llewellyn, the same aunt who'd rescued my mother from boarding school, enrolled me in two extra-curricular activities, ballet and piano, probably to help me along. During the ballet class, performing delicate movements made me feel clumsy and self-conscious. After my aunt and mother saw the Christmas performance, no one asked me to continue.

I took but one piano lesson. In it the instructor played middle "C" and a few other notes. Then he held a piece of shirt cardboard between my eyes and the keys and said to play what he'd played. *What*? I said to myself, too shy to ask out loud, ***I can't find them if I can't see; what's he doing***? I was so distressed I begged not to have more lessons, even though I wanted terribly to learn to play like my mother. It wasn't until a couple of years ago in an "aha" moment that I understood: the instructor intended me to use hearing to find the notes... not memory.

At the end of third grade, I finally succeeded in joining a group! At recess I saw several girls, maybe thirty, form a large circle around a lone girl in the center. The school bell rang, recess was over and yet they didn't move. Overcome with curiosity, I went over and said to a couple of them, "What's happening?" "We can't tell you. You'd tell." I replied, "I won't tell; you can trust me." But they insisted, "No, we can't!"

With my integrity questioned, I became indignant. For possibly the first time in a social setting, the vise that normally disabled my tongue loosened. I stated clearly in an earnest but defiant voice, "You certainly can trust me!" They said, "Then OK, come," and allowed me to form part of the circle.

I was astonished: the girl in the center had soiled her pants, and the others were acting as her protectors. Today I muse over that helpful response the group made. The poor girl was too embarrassed to go to a teacher to say what had happened, but with so many playmates ignoring the bell the teacher had to come outdoors, discover the problem and lead the girl away to get cleaned up.

My bravery–insisting that the group accept me–both surprised and pleased me. But, although my classmates accepted me that one time, school soon ended for the year and

I couldn't practice being part of the group on a regular basis. That might have helped me learn to talk about everyday things, which was what I needed most.

☙

By age six I found some comfort in my backyard. I learned that everything there grew and changed in ways that made sense. Overhead I watched varieties of birds tweet and twerp and I marveled at their wings that carried them wherever they wanted to go. When I sat, I examined hundreds of tiny insects crawling purposefully to destinations. I was amazed to be able to make whistles with long blades of green grass.

It wasn't all rosy in the backyard. In my mother's many little gardens I smelled pretty flowers and watched buds blossom grandly and later die. If I picked something, I knew it would be dead the next day. It caused me to think the whole world might be arbitrary. It was kind of frightening because the Sunday school teachers and my parents taught me the earth and all its creatures functioned within a carefully thought-out system. Yet I felt better in my backyard than in any other place, and I especially enjoyed the turtles I caught.

One of the many things my father built for me was a wire fence around our little pond so my turtles couldn't get away. When I wanted to see one, I retrieved it with a long-handled net and set it on my palm, which I flattened out like a platform. The turtle would keep still for a long time, not moving in the slightest. Then, if I kept very quiet, it would slowly, very, very slowly, poke out its long, thin neck, thus allowing me to study its markings. I couldn't believe the intricacy of the designs, especially those of the Eastern Pond red-eared variety.

Each little turtle head, even the smallest, seemed to have hundreds of tiny lines and wrinkles. The skin on their necks overlapped when their heads were hidden, but when they stretched their necks to see something, the skin elongated. I thought turtles were extremely special because they grew their houses on their backs and could tuck in their extremities when threatened. Their teeny black eyes, no bigger than a speck of dirt, could see everything; they saw me coming from far away and in no time at all plunged into the water.

Their complex abilities astonished me. They lived and breathed in water and out of it; they could both swim and walk. They could walk as slowly as only a turtle could, but when something startled them, they dashed to safety like a cat. When it was cold, they could burrow under the mud, sleep and breathe so slowly that they didn't need food or much air.

How I wished I were a turtle and could hide so easily! When I was in school I had to stay visible, stand with my long arms and big hands hanging down by my sides and in front of me for everyone to notice and see I had no one to play with. Many times I wanted to be out of sight, but I couldn't disappear like a turtle.

☙

My father, tall with grayish-white hair and good-looking, always seemed to have a suntan. He tended to be in a good mood and to keep active. I don't remember seeing him sitting down accept during lunch on weekends.

At six o'clock I usually waited near the front door to be there when he drove up in his Model A Ford coupe from the train station. He would give me a warm greeting and, once in a rare while, bring me a statue of a horse he would buy at Grand Central Station. My horse collection was my greatest treasure.

I thought horses were the most magnificent animals on earth and to see them I watched every western movie possible on our four-inch television. The Lone Ranger's horse, Silver, was my favorite, followed by Roy Rogers' Trigger. I seldom saw a real horse up close and it never occurred to me that I might own one someday.

On weekends, my father sometimes worked in the backyard making our place beautiful and building things for us kids. He built several tree huts and a three-story playhouse that must have been at least twenty feet high. I didn't play much in it or in the tree-houses–they were lonely places without playmates.

When I was about seven, I fondly recall my father taking me aside to teach me lessons. "Never run while you're carrying something sharp because if you fall, it could cut you. When you carry scissors, hold them away from you, like this," and he held his arm way out to one side. Another time he warned me not to cut my hand between the thumb and forefinger for fear of getting lockjaw. He described that as not being able to open my mouth and not being able to eat anything. I was happy to learn how to avoid that!

He also painstakingly showed me how to dump things into our river in such a manner I wouldn't fall in and drown. He gave me a bushel basket of leaves to empty according to his instruction, "Don't bend over while you do it, even though it's natural to do. The weight of the falling leaves will pull you down. Watch me. Stand up straight and hold the basket away from you and then turn it upside down." To practice, I dumped out leaves both ways, away from the river. I felt so happy and knowledgeable.

My father seemed to possess a wealth of information and I would have delighted in knowing more, but had to content myself with what he offered me. I knew he didn't want to be interrupted while he worked in the woodshed, because when I asked him a question, quite often he'd say, "Wait, Helen, I can't talk while I'm doing this." But times to talk rarely materialized.

The information about carrying sharp objects, avoiding lockjaw and understanding inertia was about the only practical knowledge I received from my parents to prepare me for life. There were many moments growing up and afterward when I desperately needed guidance and because I didn't receive it I tripped up frequently. Not knowing what to do amplified my sense of inferiority, which in turn fueled my shyness.

ଓ

My wonderful and only grandmother, Nana, entertained. She made people of all ages feel good, including one quiet little girl. She was short and for that reason didn't appear as threatening as a tall adult could. She smiled a lot, too, using her pretty blue eyes as well as her wide, thin mouth, causing everyone around her to light up. She wore child-friendly clothes, pale blue dresses with white, happy-looking critters on them that often seemed as jovial as she. When she spoke to you, she invited responses.

As a young bride, Nana may have acquiesced to her husband's wishes that servants bring up their children, but after he died in 1933, she spent lots of time with her grandchildren. All ten of us have raved about her care when she looked after us in times of need.

In order to help my mother, Nana lived near us at a hotel in Greenwich from November through April, until we moved to Prince Edward Island when I was nine. The hotel was a huge, three- or four-story white building constructed in the grand old style with wide, gray verandas dotted with white wicker furniture with white and green striped canvas upholstery. I thought she was living in a castle and was enchanted. Nana often took me to the hotel to provide tranquility for my mother, and, fortunately for me, being with her relieved me from the tensions of loneliness I experienced at home and in school.

I often spent whole weekends at the hotel and sometimes visited during the week for a special reason, such as getting my hair cut. Then she would pick me up from school and we'd go straight to the beauty parlor. I hated having my hair cut; the very idea produced powerful feelings of personal violation. But Nana stood near me while the beautician clipped, making the ordeal less traumatic.

When I visited, she had a cot for me to sleep on in her room and a card table set up. We spent entire afternoons playing card games she taught me: two-person solitaire, many kinds of rummy including Oklahoma, and my favorite, canasta. By the time I was four, we played it using four decks and I was overjoyed to manipulate twenty-six cards at a time. Nana also taught me songs by singing them repetitively, and one time I laughingly persuaded her to sing "Onward Christian Soldiers" ten times in a row while we were out driving.

I liked to go out to the large lawns to play, and Nana allowed me the joyous freedom to do so by myself. I discovered an abandoned railroad track out behind the hotel. On both sides of the tracks a few small, decaying wooden buildings remained with rusted iron pipes sticking out like broken fingers. A tangle of vines and tall weeds climbed and snaked into a canopy of leafy trees overhead, forming a perfect setting for a play place.

One day I invited Nana to see it. She came in her usual dress: leather shoes, silk stockings, a pretty coat with a sable collar and one of the dark-colored hats she wore when she went out. I hoped the thistles wouldn't damage her stockings.

A few feet in front of her, I turned, and with some trepidation, looked up at her to ask, "Is this place OK?" "Yes," she said, beaming at me with unabashed enthusiasm, and I knew right then for certain Nana would do anything in the world for me. It was so marvelous not to be bored, to have fun, to have a loving person excited to be doing things with me.

Nana could be stern as well. She'd always told me to wash using a soapy facecloth. One afternoon, I decided to play a joke. After washing, I squeezed out every spec of moisture from my facecloth to trick her into thinking I didn't use it. When she complained, I said, "Oh, but I did use it... I just wrung it out so much it seems like I didn't." Well, when Nana heard this, I guess she thought it was a fib, because I couldn't convince her I'd really used it. Making me feel ashamed, she scolded me over and over until I knew I would never try anything like that again.

Even my eating problems vanished at Nana's: in the dining room I could select anything I wanted. I always had the same: fried sole, peas, mashed potato and chocolate ice cream. Nana did the ordering, because even with her, I never felt brave enough to speak with anyone else.

Every single evening, when the waiter, Ralph, a black man from the South, cleared the main course plates, he chided me by asking, "Do you want strawberry ice cream for dessert?" forcing me to blurt out, "No, chocolate!"

He would bend backwards and forwards laughing while Nana smiled at his game that made me speak. In a way, they were recognizing my shyness, and, in a way, I appreciated it. Nevertheless a part of me cringed. The warm feeling of commiseration was good, but it reminded me of my pervasive fear of people, and that wasn't funny.

Nana did try to get me used to people. When others were around, she would keep me right up front, by hooking her arm in mine. I stood still, but I hated it and my fear of talking didn't lessen.

Although I would be tired and happy when she drove me home, I always studied my parents' expressions to see if they'd missed me, to find out what had happened while I was away, to see if I'd been gypped, like the time I discovered that my parents and Nat had gone to a wedding without me. My need to be recognized and loved by my parents was fundamental–the best grandmothering in the world couldn't diminish that.

Every June, my family drove to Crescent Surf in Kennebunk, Maine, where my mother's family had summered for fifty years. We stayed with Nana for three weeks. I didn't have her all to myself the way I did at the hotel, but in addition to allowing me to eat what I liked, she planned activities for my whole family, thereby guaranteeing that I, too, had things to do, including playing on the beach. I was seldom lonely.

The beach was littered with life: snails, sand dollars, razor fish, and the rarest and most exciting of all, horseshoe crabs. Baby crabs nestled in the dozens of tidal pools surrounding the hundreds of huge boulders that began at Nana's beach and ended in front of Aunt Llewellyn's house. I memorized where the best rocks were for stepping on, so I could run the entire stretch without stopping, imagining myself a wild animal and feeling wonderful.

ঔ

By age seven, I sometimes misbehaved deliberately. I would nag my mother over and over about something, such as "Mom, when can I have a Fudgsicle?"—until she couldn't stand it. I knew I could outwit her: she didn't think as fast as I. And in some instances, she wasn't as strong physically. When she laid me on her lap to hit me with a hairbrush, I could twist my arm around, grab her wrist and hold her at bay.

She couldn't figure out how to punish me when my father was at work. At times—not often—she called my father in New York to come home to discipline me, to put me in my room, since I now ran off when she tried to do it herself.

I learned how to stall her from contacting my father at work. We had two telephones, one upstairs and one down, and while she dialed on one I could run fast enough to the other one to lift up the receiver and break the connection. For several moments, while I panted and scrambled up and down the steep staircase, my emotions swung back and forth between sheer terror and pure delight. Eventually my mother won out, of course, but I succeeded in creating a fuss. My father would hardly look at me when he arrived from New York—rather, he concerned himself with soothing my mother's frayed nerves.

I didn't feel the same shame over this as when Nana had scolded me about the facecloth. It was more like getting back at my parents for not treating me better. I sulked over their reactions to my naughtiness; I knew they should be asking me my why I misbehaved, allowing me to express myself. Although I might have been too shy to talk about it, I sure would have liked to have been asked. In many ways, I was on my own with my parents, and I didn't like it.

ᘓ

At age eight, my parents still shut me in my room, I had no one to play with, and I started dreading the future, wondering what was in store for me. I enjoyed being outdoors, but I began to see problems: I understood instinctively I was a part of nature, just like the turtles, but they seemed to know how to develop. I did not. I knew I had to grow and change, but I couldn't understand what growing up entailed. I feared the worst, such as my aged caregivers dying and leaving me stranded.

By the time I was nine, my fear of the future became scarier. Once when I was alone in bed, half asleep, trying to envision my life beyond age fourteen for the umpteenth time, I felt as if a huge, dark navy blue curtain was coming down on top of me, suffocating me.

A few weeks later I was reminded of my powerlessness again when Nat was about to have his tonsils removed. For the first time, my mother explained something to Nat and me together, making the topic foreboding and important: "Sometimes the doctor can't make you well at home and you have to go to a special place called a hospital to get better." She went on, "Nat's going to one tomorrow to have an operation and then he'll be better." It felt strange for my mother to prep me about operations even though it was only Nat who needed one. Nat looked uneasy.

He left for the hospital with both of my parents and I stayed behind with a babysitter. Just a few hours later, my parents woke me thumping up the stairwell. In a weary but matter-of-fact tone, my mother, sighed, "Nat screamed so much the doctor decided not to operate." Under my blankets, my thoughts raced. ***Nat sure knows how to get what he wants—even now when he's sick. Look at how he got his way with all those adults. And me, I wore braces on my arms by myself behind a locked door.*** Those thoughts disturbed me so much my mind shut down and became numb for a few moments.

For decades after that, when someone would make a remark that unnerved me, similar waves of numbing emotions prevented me from being in the moment. I would turn my head away from the threatening person, barely remembering a thing said. Fortunately, this phenomenon happened rarely, but when it did, my detached state kept me from addressing the hurtful remarks, making me feel incapable.

During the Cos Cob years I was only happy at Nana's. I can't recall good times, smiling times at home. The saying, "What you don't know won't hurt you" isn't true. I didn't experience much joy or love as a child and I was pretty darned certain I was missing something. I was getting more and more disturbed from feeling lonely and insecure when my parents made a surprising announcement. My father was retiring early, at age sixty, and because he wanted to enjoy farm life, we were moving to Prince Edward Island. I'm not quite sure why, but I had hope for a better existence. For one thing, my parents told me I could have a horse, I couldn't wait! And I may have just plain felt relief to leave the home and school where I'd found so little joy.

3

The Island, 1951–1955: What's in a Horse?

I was overjoyed when I saw the beautiful horse. She was to be my very own. About nine, my age, I named her Jenny and right away asked my father all about her and how she compared with the other horses in Hampton, the village where I now lived. "She's part Percheron and part Morgan, which makes her on the small side, but she's sure-footed and good for riding. Most important, she'll be gentle and good-natured. The other horses in town are bigger, much heavier and only used for working."

My father held his palms together to form a stirrup, and with a heave, I was on her. The joy of being on a horse was even more perfect than I'd imagined. I was up higher than even my father and I could see forever. My father led her by the reins for a few minutes, instructing me how to say "giddy-up" and "whoa." Afterward I rode her around slowly by myself. She was as gentle and obedient as could be.

I combed her coarse, wavy black mane and tail with a currycomb until they were fluffy, and brushed her multihued brown coat until it shone. I learned where her ticklish spots were: under her mouth, below her ears, and especially above her hind legs near her stomach, where her fur thinned out and the color matched the light tan of her nose. I loved the pungent, husk-like smell of her rounded back and the strength of her supple neck. Sometimes when Jenny stood still, I hung by her neck just to show myself how very strong she was.

Jenny's ears spoke for her. When they were up, she was happy; when they were straight back, she was mad. When she was scared, her ears turned around, her eyes turned fiery and her nostrils broadened; nevertheless, while in this state of fear, she never lurched suddenly, causing me to fall off. Instead, when she sensed a snake or something unusual in the grass, she signaled danger with a rapid twitch of her ears and several up and down movements of her head, and I knew to let her step away from the scary area. I liked to hear her exchange whinnies with other horses as I rode by them.

ꝏ

In 1951, many Americans had never heard of Prince Edward Island, an hour's ride from New Brunswick on an icebreaking ferry that carried over a hundred cars and even the train. Smaller than Rhode Island, the original immigrants called it the Garden of the Gulf, and the 100,000 current inhabitants called it P.E.I., or the Island.

Crescent shaped, the Island divides the warm waters of the Northumberland Straits on the south from the cold Gulf of St. Lawrence on the north. Aside from two modest-sized cities, most people lived in a couple hundred scattered villages. Hampton, with its 125 people, mostly farmers, lay on the south.

During my first summer on our farm, I spent some time riding Jenny near the border of our property watching men with big equipment spread black tar on top of the red clay road, turning it into the first paved highway on the Island. It was an important development, especially because the Canadian government paid to keep it open in the winter. The local towns had never plowed their roads, and in winter people had to travel on foot or by horse and sleigh, keeping life insular and making access to medical help or fresh food difficult.

For two hundred years, rural life had changed little and people still used kerosene lamps, woodstoves, hand-operated water pumps, as well as outdated equipment for the Island's two industries, farming and fishing. The fishermen eked out a steady livelihood, but the farmers' plight seesawed depending on weather and the market for potatoes, their main crop. Often they made too little, and during my nine years there, three middle-aged farmers I knew by name committed suicide because of economic distress.

ঔ

On a family vacation, my parents had fallen in love with the Island and with one farm in particular. Although it had no rivers, brooks or ponds like our home in Cos Cob, it was on a hill and the view of the Northumberland Straits stretched as far as the eye could see in both directions. An offer was made and accepted.

My parents named the farm Crowfield. Consisting of many buildings, all but four—the house, woodshed, barn and a floorless shed—sagged beyond repair. It took a few minutes to ride Jenny at a trot across the width of our farm and more than ten to reach the woods in back of our house. In front, across the highway, someone else owned a large field that sloped to the saltwater marsh. Surrounded by scrub bushes and thin spruce, ducks and geese took shelter on it during migrations.

Bleached cedar shingles covered the two-and-a-half-story gambrel-roofed barn, built for several dozen cattle and up to eight horses. A long, narrow, faded-red woodshed contained space for carpentry workshops, a garage and pens for smaller animals. Our geese slept in the building with the dirt floor. A lot of horse-related equipment came with the farm: a driving sleigh, a wood sleigh, a dump cart, a truck wagon and a two-seated buggy or driving carriage. My father taught me to harness Jenny and hitch her to each vehicle. We had both English and Western saddles, although I usually rode bareback.

The house lacked electricity, plumbing, a telephone and a furnace, and during the first couple of months, before we modernized everything, my mother used to say it was like camping. I liked our three living rooms: the den where we watched television; the front room where we listened to classical music on a record player and the big room where we did everything else. Its pretty floral wallpaper matched the only adornment that came with the house: an antique kerosene lamp that hung in the middle of the room on a brass chain connected to the beautiful, molded, white tin ceiling.

The lamp's two-foot-wide, pale green porcelain dome, shaped like an open parachute, rested on a glass chimney and a brass base that held fuel. Eventually my father learned to avoid banging his head on it.

☙

My father wasn't a big talker, but his kind smile and friendliness won him the locals' respect even though he never wore the customary attire–blue jeans and plaid shirts–preferring instead a lightweight shirt, tie, opened suit jacket and slacks. He asked the neighbors for advice about farming and bartered with one for hay and fencing in exchange for using some of our land. The villagers didn't feel threatened economically by him because he never sold anything but a little cream.

After buying two horses, one for Nat and one for me, he busied himself selecting cows, steers and heifers. He chose Jerseys because their milk is so tasty. In those days people didn't know to limit fatty foods, so we poured generous amounts of thick, yellow cream on cereals and desserts.

We all became involved in choosing the smaller animals: a lamb, laying hens, ducks, geese, turkeys and guinea hens. Once the guinea hens disappeared and no one knew where they'd gone until one Sunday morning in church, while my mother played the organ and everyone sang, they started squawking in the basement. I liked all the animals, but after Jenny, I thought the tall-necked Chinese geese were striking. They had perfectly round black knobs on their foreheads and I thrilled watching them stride from their house with yellow, fluffy goslings running to keep up.

Crowfield was a hobby farm, a dream come true for my father who yearned to practice his brand of Unitarian philosophy, that of simple living in the country. It may be difficult for urban people today to understand just how much work he willingly took on. For the cows and horses alone, in addition to feeding them year-round, during the long winters he shoveled out the stalls and put down fresh straw bedding daily, leaving the barn smelling fresh. But his philosophy wasn't all about physical labor.

He spent the afternoons indoors, in the big room, sitting in the Quaker rocker, first reading the classics and then listening to the big wooden radio. When he talked about the farm, his hazel brown eyes lit up below his broad forehead and balding head (which he tried to cover by combing a few strands of straight white hair to one side).

But the twinkle in his eyes never shone brighter than during the afternoons when my mother played lively music on the piano. With no provocation, he would toss up his arms like a ballet dancer and twirl around, doing a two-step across our living room floor (avoiding the lamp) on his way to the kitchen, to the rhythm of his own atonal voice singing one of the oldies he loved such as, "East side, west side, all around the town, when you have a Manhattan take a Bronx to wash it down."

My father's presence added enormous comfort for me. Unlike in Cos Cob, my door was never locked and my father ate with us three times a day. No one ever told me to finish my plate or eat something I didn't like. In hindsight, his being at home all day must have alleviated my mother's worry about disciplining Nat and me, thus making conditions better for her, too.

Part of my life had improved: I could rise in the morning, dash out to a barnyard of animals and ride Jenny. However, I knew the joy I derived from her and the other animals wasn't a substitute for friendships with girls, and it disappointed me that no one mentioned my social anxieties. Soon though, that changed.

ɷ

One day during our first summer in Hampton, my mother walked the half-mile to town with me. On the way home, I saw two girls about my size staring at us from the middle of a large field of red dirt. Although I couldn't distinguish their faces, I could tell by their wistful glances they were curious to know me. Ah, I thought, maybe P.E.I. will be okay and I'll be able to talk.

I didn't get to know those two girls until school started—and never walked again to town with my mother. However, when my parents drove to a few farms to get acquainted with people, I met two other girls. One, Margaret, was five years older than I; she lived beside the water, down a mile-long, narrow sandy lane on a farm with slumping gray buildings. After my mother mentioned my horse, Margaret offered to take me for a ride on Queenie, their farm horse. With someone's help, I mounted a horse as high as a door, with a rump as large as a card table. Accustomed to hauling heavy equipment, Queenie maintained a boring, steady pace.

People in Hampton didn't ride horses, and after experiencing Queenie's lumbering gait, I understood why. Instead they used those huge animals to plow fields, haul dump carts and transport logs on wood sleighs. As a girl, my affection for our smaller horses was accepted, and eventually some girls even came to our farm to ride my horse with me.

Although my parents visited neighbors that first year, no one from Hampton ever came to see us, or from what I could tell, even stopped by to visit one another. Perhaps their socializing took place at church and in the two general stores. But since my parents continued to make visits that first summer, on another day I met Marjorie and a stallion.

A red-haired, heavily freckled girl three or four years older than I, Marjorie lived about a mile inland from the new highway on one of the bigger farms in town. There were piles of manure outside, all around the barn, but inside a mighty, dappled gray Percheron stallion with almost black legs and trim feet captured my imagination. The stallion's thick gray-white mane was far longer than my arm and it and his tail swished high and wide while he snorted and swung nervously from side to side in his box stall. He seldom went outdoors for any purpose other than an encounter with a female.

I overheard Marjorie's brothers allude to those wildly engaging moments, and though Marjorie said she peeked once, she said it wasn't something women were allowed to see. I thought how lucky she was to live there and be able to sneak up and look. Once I walked to this farm by myself, but only once, because I had nothing to do but stand around and watch Marjorie scrub clothes. No one seemed to have any free time for entertainment of any sort. To my dismay, I soon learned each family busied itself almost solely with chores. Margaret and Marjorie no longer went to school, so I hardly ever saw them again.

I had no chores, so I stood out. In Cos Cob I'd felt different because of my silence and not knowing how to play;

here my lifestyle differed from everyone else's in town. I lived in a beautifully decorated, centrally heated home with many forms of entertainment, including books, a television and music. A maid cleaned our home and did the laundry.

Some say rural Island folk are quiet and gentle, and my experience bears this out. I couldn't have moved to a more conducive environment to start talking. I could stand around, say nothing and blend in because no one spoke much. But there was seldom much I wanted to say. I didn't want to discuss what I did at home because it was so unusual for them: they didn't have electricity, let alone televisions or radios and they didn't play games or read. I probably tackled the "I'm different" dilemma in the best way, by trying to ignore it, but of course it didn't go away. For certain, I was delighted to be accepted, to be able to talk, but I wasn't at all excited over the villagers' lifestyle, which consisted of little but work.

I learned to talk like the others—quickly, using sparse monosyllabic words. I didn't learn fundamentals of good conversation or how to exchange ideas. I used some of these skills at home, but I always could there—my difficulty had always occurred trying to communicate outside my family.

But we did share one topic with the villagers, the weather. It daunted us all and provided an easy, perennial conversation. I enjoyed having this interest in common with everyone, and today I suspect the Islanders liked it, too.

ശ

The Canadian government encouraged births and education by providing a monthly allowance of up to thirty dollars for each child until age fourteen, as long as they attended school.

About forty children attended Hampton Elementary School, all under the age of fifteen.

The faded yellow, two-room schoolhouse, an outhouse and a pile of wood sat on an acre of land several feet back from the new paved highway. In exchange for a small salary, an older pupil carried in wood, chopped kindling and lit fires in the two stoves—one in each room—and once in a while, swept the dull gray-brown hardwood floors.

Water came from a long-handled pump located in the hallway that led to the elementary room. Rows of windows on two sides of each room provided the only source of light. A sense of history oozed from names and initials long since carved into the two-seater desks. To the left of the school, a rickety, creaky door opened into a rancid smelling outhouse with outdated catalogues from Eaton's department store for toilet paper.

None of those antiquated conditions bothered me, but within a few days I was mortified by everyone's behavior; I couldn't see a glimpse of inspiration for learning in anyone, not even in the teacher! Over time this bothered me in a subliminal way, because I couldn't understand it and had no control over it. What did I, a ten-year-old, think? That this school was useless, pathetic, a waste of time, boring? I'm not sure what I thought, but I went to school like children do, with no say in it. For sure, though, it didn't seem like an education because I didn't feel as if I were learning.

In the whole village there were only four girls around my age. The parents of two of them kept them at home doing chores when not in school, but I got to know the other two, the girls I'd seen in the field at the beginning of the summer. Gloria was my senior by two years and Edith a year younger.

It was a tremendous relief to have these two peers, even though we had little in common except our gender, age and proximity. By fall they rode with me and we slept over at each other's homes.

I don't remember much about Gloria, except she was the only one who had a real interest in riding. Then, after a couple of years, without a word to me, she moved to Toronto with a much older boyfriend. Although people were desperate to leave the Island and its hardships—which was joked about frequently—few were brave enough to do it. Gloria, by doing it when only fourteen, made me see just how anxious people were to get away. I didn't know what I wanted, but going to the big city at that age was not it.

Shorter than I, but with a body that promised to be curvy, Edith did nothing unusual when she and I played, and nothing our parents might object to in the least: when we weren't riding Jenny, we sat for a bit, talking very little, hardly at all, and then she went home. She rode with little enthusiasm, but never said no when I invited her. I didn't feel inferior or self-conscious with her, and when I chose to speak, I wasn't too nervous about it.

The nights I spent at her house taught me how farmers really lived. I'm sure our house and customs appeared just as strange to her as theirs to me, but it was so new and exciting for me to have any form of social life that these exchange visits may have been more memorable for me than for her.

Edith's house was large, yet the only source of heat came from a wood-burning kitchen range that had a tank on the side to heat water for washing. At mealtime, her family of five and I ate not far from it, in the small dining room off the kitchen. In it there was a window, a couple of unframed pictures from an old calendar and a framed image of Christ. A faded red-and-white-check oilcloth covered a square table surrounded by eight straight-backed wooden chairs.

For dinner, taken at noon, we passed around a cake-sized mixing bowl filled with boiled potatoes. Each person prepared these on his or her plate by peeling, mashing and then glazing them with varying amounts of butter, salt and pepper.

Talk, usually accompanied by a hearty grin, was scarce and often habitual, such as, "Joey likes a heavy dose of pepper on his potatoes," "Ruthie mashes her potatoes flatter than anyone," and "Snider coats his with lots of butter." This social milieu suited me fine; it required a mere smile, something I could handle, and the potatoes tasted fine.

In addition to the mashed white staple, we had beef that had been tenderized by hours of boiling, soft canned vegetables, and a generous stack of incomparably delicious homemade white bread. I wished my mother baked it so its aroma would permeate our house. Suppers were usually leftovers from dinner fried up with a little onion, followed by dessert.

In the Scottish tradition, Edith's family ate many sweets. I remember coconut macaroons, unbelievable shortbreads, chocolate oatmeal balls with coconut, lemon meringue tarts and apple, lemon and rhubarb pies. Even with eating so much sugar, it seemed people brushed their teeth not to avoid decay but only as a means to clean their breath. I say this because their toothbrushes were so old the bristles had flattened into unique sculpted shapes, none of which resembled a brush.

Edith and I gorged ourselves with sweets and tea before going to bed, a frantic event in cold months. After leaving the warm kitchen, we rushed upstairs, jumped into our pajamas, blew out the portable kerosene lamp and burrowed under piles of colorful, handmade quilts that saved us from freezing in the non-insulated, unheated bedroom. Inevitably, we leapt up in the night to relieve ourselves of the tea in the china chamber pot stored under the bed. In the morning, we dressed and dashed to the kitchen where Edith's mother tended a blazing fire.

Water and cleanliness, though never a matter of much discussion or significance in my house—we had indoor plumbing and paid someone to clean—required mammoth energy at the neighbors'. Sometimes I watched Edith kneel on the floor and wash a huge pile of clothes in a big aluminum tub with a washboard. With no running water, they used small amounts for piles of laundry and I wondered whether clothes rinsed with dirty water would be clean or dirty when they dried. I wasn't fussy, I just wondered about it. Before eating, everyone cleaned their hands in a small tin basin with a red rim using the same water; I didn't like being last because by then the water was brown.

☙

In many ways I appreciated my home not just because I had Jenny, but also because of the activities we did as a family, such as bridge and various table games like Go. When not listening to the news on the radio or watching regular television programs such as Ed Sullivan and *Leave It to Beaver*, we often talked about worldly happenings we'd seen in the *National Geographic* magazine. We didn't go anywhere as a family, there being no place to go—the general store delivered groceries, so we didn't have the chance even to shop together. All our interests were centered in the home.

I'd compare the conversations between my girlfriends and their mothers, about everyday work and social concerns, such as how to respond to a comment someone made, with the discussions in my home. We didn't express our thoughts about relationships. Our personal thoughts were about our interests: my mother, her gardens or what was she reading; my father, the news or the animals; Nat, hunting; and I, Jenny. We never talked about my anxieties or my growing up. The insecurity I felt from not knowing what I should do stoked my shyness.

Nat spent much of his time in his bedroom and occupied himself with hobbies such as stuffing birds and making flies for fishing. He didn't ride his horse after it threw him off or have much to do with the farm. We walked to school separately; maybe he thought it unmanly to walk with his little sister. At first I wished I didn't have to walk by myself.

We had few visitors, and no one came to hear my mother play the piano. I desperately wanted her to teach me how to play, but we ended up bickering. Frustrated from not understanding her instructions, I complained, "You're not teaching me right!" She looked straight ahead at the piano and, to my huge disappointment, said, "I'm doing all I know how to."

For rainy days I had few hobbies, so I often stayed in the same room with my mother. She gave me things to do, such as looking at pictures she thought I would like in a magazine, listening to symphonic records or holding a skein of yarn while she wrapped it into a ball.

She taught me how to knit, and I made a thick gray cardigan with a large pink eagle on the back. I wore it so proudly–it was my symbol to the townspeople that I did the same sorts of things with my mother that other children did with theirs. The truth was, and the townsfolk probably knew it as well as I did, that my mother and I differed from the other females in town so much that we had almost nothing in common.

My father taught me how to hunt birds, something no other girls did. "Always have your gun pointed at the ground near your feet. When you see a bird"—he paused—"lift it up slowly, like this, making sure no one's in your range, and cock it. Hold it steady against your shoulder and shoot when the bird's just overhead." Then one dark October morning we went hunting, I carrying my own 12-gauge shotgun. For fifteen minutes we trod lightly to the marsh so the birds wouldn't hear us and fly off before we settled in a blind to wait for the sun to come up. After two exciting hours of looking, we returned empty-handed. I treasured this special outing with my father, although I didn't discuss it with my friends because they would think it strange.

ꭥ

When I was eleven, I entered the school's big room, the one for the "big" kids. The teacher suggested that I skip the sixth grade and go into the seventh, because she thought I needed more demanding material. However, what she chose for me to study didn't excite me, and learning continued to be as boring as it had been in grades four and five. Edith remained in the other room and we didn't see each other.

The older girls paid me little attention. At recess and at lunchtime they crowded together, sitting on desktops, talking about boyfriends and activities outside of school. I listened awkwardly.

Generally, I had been low down in the pecking order, but now, much more so. Many boys teased me, making fun of me on a daily basis by calling me "baggy" because of my oversized blue jeans. I presume in order to save money, my mother tended to buy me clothing that was too large, "to allow me room to grow into it," and I was too shy to ask her not to do that.

One day at home during dinner, I believe in an effort to help, Nat began to say how the kids joked about me at school. My mother flashed him a look that said, "We don't talk about that," which silenced him.

Perhaps she thought it would make me feel uncomfortable. But just the opposite occurred: my heart leapt in the hope that relief might be at hand. I needed someone to talk with about my hurts, and I couldn't muster the courage to say so on my own. It felt dreadful that my mother appeared uninterested in learning how I fared at school. The mockery ruined my school life, where I hated to stand up and walk because people could see my baggy pants. The next school year I fared better; those boys turned fifteen and dropped out because they were too old to get the government allowance.

ଓ

Once a week my family and I attended the United Church of Canada. Prior to the service, I went to Sunday School and, unlike elementary school, this did cause me to use my mind, though not along the lines the minister would have hoped.

While on my horse, I thought about nature, religion and philosophy to the extent my youthful mind could. The Bible stories they read to us in Sunday school and the hymns we sang perplexed me. Did God really count each sparrow that fell? Did He actually know how many grains of sand the beaches contained in the whole world? Did He care for everybody and know what each person did simultaneously? And finally, purely from my imagination I asked, did God love me more than He loved my horse?

I was stunned by the realization that I, and therefore every person in the world, could meddle with God's world in an arbitrary fashion. When I rode Jenny she stepped on insects that would die. Was there a God somewhere waiting to see where I would take my horse and then count the insects she walked on? What about wars, illnesses and all kinds of cruelty?

I realized I couldn't solve the God dilemma, so I stopped thinking about it, though I went to church because everybody did. I wondered if others believed that God cared for all living creatures, but nobody at church ever spoke about Him and I couldn't tell. I didn't discuss these questions with my parents and I didn't overhear them or Nat discuss their religious beliefs.

☙

But my spirit survived being friendless, confused and awash in school, because nature and Jenny provided refuge. In particular, I loved the challenges of winter, with its lengthy blizzards characterized by subzero temperatures, high snowbanks, slippery ice and the tantalizing swirling winds. I felt at one with nature.

Even in storms I walked the mile to school, and to go home for lunch, I did the trek twice. I was the only girl who lived west of the village, so for that part of the way, I walked alone. I loved snow eddying around my eyes, nose and neck and of wind billowing my jacket and pants while treading the partially plowed, treacherous highway. I felt alive, strong and fearless.

In those winters I cherished taking Jenny out. Unable to walk in several feet of snow, she leapt and sprang through it, making hanging on difficult. To do so, from inside wool mittens made slippery by caked snow, I wound my small fingers into her mane and squeezed my short legs around her bare circular sides with all my might, allowing me to feel brave and strong. I never fell off into the powdery, deep snow, although sometimes I thought it might be hard to get home if I did.

I enjoyed the best feeling of potency while driving the long, heavy wood sleigh. Designed to haul logs out of the woods, it was knee-high and flat on top with nothing on it except four posts, one on each corner, positioned there to contain logs. With nothing to sit on, I stood, guiding Jenny using long black leather reins, with wind created by her brisk gait beating against my face and chest. Then when we encountered small snow-banks, the sleigh lunged up and down, forcing me to crouch on bended knees while swaying from one leg to the other to avoid falling off. Every muscle I owned worked to keep me steady, providing a joyous respite for my mind so often beset with social anxiety.

For pure pleasure, after a snowfall I'd ride in the driving sleigh with a fur blanket on my lap, listening to soft, muted sounds of my horse's hooves as she trotted languidly on the snowy pavement. The sun bounced off snow that blanketed everything–fields, branches, electricity wires. It was so perfect I felt as if I were in a movie.

In warm weather, I rode into the Northumberland Straits. When the water became deep enough for Jenny to swim, her legs, proportionately small in comparison to her body, thrashed like full throttled pistons in order to keep her afloat. These motions made her too bumpy to ride, so I floated beside her, holding on firmly to her mane, ever alert to jump back on before her feet touched the sand or else she would gallop away without me. I felt nimble as Tarzan.

ଔ

In my isolated village, gossip could be called the book of life or the means to survive. It stitched people together and helped make their lives interesting as well as serving specific purposes. Few supplies were store-bought, even medicines, so women compared the efficacy of their homemade remedies. I never heard of improper sexual behavior—no one stayed in town if they intended to break mores. No one could afford to be affected or rude. People scrutinized how others spent money and how hard they worked. Not caring personally about the lives and habits of the 125 townspeople, their talk had never much concerned me.

But now I was getting older. And, in grade eight, when Edith entered the big room with Della, we became a threesome. I hadn't known Della well; she never rode with me. She was more Edith's friend, but one day on the way home from school, she invited me in for supper.

She lived with her parents and two older brothers in a small house in the center of town, beside the service station, across from the church that perched on a steep little hill. Della wasn't especially pretty, smart or special in any way I could see. Her father and an older brother earned meager incomes from jobs in far away Charlottetown. At supper her quiet, slender father received the only portion of meat, a small one, and the rest of us ate one ear of tough, deep-yellow corn. Afterward, Della and her short, plump mother, Cora, and I sat in the front porch where, for a few minutes, we quietly watched the cars go by.

Then Cora turned and looked at me. "You shouldn't ride horses anymore. You girls are thirteen. It's not good for young women to be interested in that. You're too old. You should be considering your future. I want Della to start looking for a husband." (Della married at fifteen. Edith shortly after. They moved away and I never heard from them again.)

I didn't question my choice. If I continued riding, gossip would ruin me. I'd struggled my entire life to have friends and didn't want to lose them because their mothers disapproved of my riding. So I stopped.

But that decision came at a price. As a result of not riding Jenny and experiencing the joys of peace and nature with her, I felt, in effect, as if I'd been cut off from my soul—I'd lost my main source of nurturing. And, being so reticent, I didn't express my disillusionment to my parents or to anyone. My troubled thoughts, unspoken and unarticulated, got burrowed and stashed within, along with my other worrisome issues, to sit it out, until much, much later when I could deal with them.

4

1954–1960:
"My God, This Place Is So Boring!"

Soon after Della's mom stopped me from riding, Nat, then fourteen, left the Island. He'd refused to do anything in school for months—wouldn't even pick up a pencil. As a consequence, my parents sent him to a private school in New Brunswick, asking me if I wanted to go, too. I imagined many interesting times happening there, such as fun conversations before bed, but my shy nature made me decline. It convinced me I wouldn't be able to make friends and fit in.

I knew Nat made the right move and that I could have gone with him, but nonetheless, once in a while I resented being left behind. At the time, I didn't comprehend the inevitable: sooner or later I'd leave, and the earlier I went, the better.

Instead, in my school I studied worn textbooks filled with pictures and large-type printing. Later on, when I was a teacher, I learned there are books of varying degrees of complexity for most subject matters and that school systems select what best suits their students. The geometry book was an exception; everyone used the same thin red classic, ***Euclid on Geometry,*** containing varying complexities of theorems. The teacher always stopped after doing five or six exercises. Each one was progressively harder, and once, feeling curious and eager to see what the ensuing problems entailed, I said, "Let's keep going!" Her jaw dropped and she glared at me. "I make the decisions here, Helen, and we're stopping now!" I looked down at my desk and couldn't think of anything else but my embarrassment until school let out that day.

Other than school and home, there was no place to go: no sports or musical events, not even movie theaters. And now, I didn't go to the barn to get my horse. I rarely went swimming or did anything else with my two girlfriends because they worked so much at home. One year someone did come from another town and taught us three girls a few sets of the Highland Fling, my only extracurricular activity.

It bothered me to have so little to do because I knew life and learning could be much more fulfilling. I remembered the stimulating exercises at Greenwich Country Day School. But, more important, for a few weeks each summer from ages ten to thirteen, I experienced an extraordinary time with my great aunt in Kennebunk, the aunt who'd helped my mother in New York as a teenager and later me in Cos Cob with ballet lessons.

During summers, Aunt Llewellyn lived in an imposing home on the ocean, a short walk from Nana's over a groomed lawn and on through an enchanting path between colorful trees. Her touched-up-with-purple hair stood above her high forehead and sprang out around her head. Short, thin and stooped, she wore loose dresses gathered at the waist with narrow belts and pretty beads that came down almost to her middle, diverting attention from her curled hands. She waved a cane, making it seem more like a wand than an instrument to keep her upright. Aunt Llewellyn's infectious laughter and exciting ideas riveted me.

My whole being crested from one exciting moment to another when she challenged, "Tell me, what do you see in this telescope?" "How you would play this bridge hand?" and "What do you think will happen in the development of mankind?" That question appealed to me in particular for I knew she was elderly and that, one day, I would continue the study of history for us both.

Once, without realizing what I was doing—without arousing my shyness—she got me to organize and host a luncheon at her house for three cousins, my age, who were visiting Crescent Surf. I didn't realize what she'd accomplished until years later.

My aunt obviously didn't understand the degree of my insular life on Prince Edward Island because for Christmas she gave me a gorgeous navy blue skirt suit with a satin collar. I had not the remotest occasion to wear it. I took it out of its box every once in a while to see how lovely it was. I didn't complain about living on Prince Edward Island to my aunt or anyone because I had pride in my family and didn't want to convey that my parents' decision to move there was ill conceived.

Then, when I was thirteen, Aunt Llewellyn died. I cried and ached, riding Jenny around and around our back fields for several weeks (out of sight of the neighbors), lamenting her death, wishing a god somewhere could have kept her alive. I stared at the sky, thinking my life was as empty and pointless as the pale clouds drifting hither and yonder. Because I had so little self-motivation or opportunities, I did nothing to continue studying the scintillating activities she'd introduced me to.

But that year biology changed me and during the winter of ninth grade, with absolutely nothing else to do, I focused on the new demands of my body.

ꕥ

Edith, Della and I provided both the backdrop and the entire stage for one another's budding adolescence. My interest in horses and nature receded, as did my wish to study and learn. I no longer found solace in my home and my parents became old-fashioned.

Being attracted to the opposite sex was intoxicating and made the sun shine just for me. I spent lots of time thinking about Gordon, a boy I liked, and many times I daydreamed about intimate scenarios with him. None of us "went all the way," but the passions that would build to it were being unleashed.

Ray, Barry and Gordon, all from a nearby village, were about the only three boys we three girls got to know and date. Well mannered and quiet-spoken, their lives seemed as limited as ours. A few years older, the sun, cold and wind from working outdoors had already reddened their complexions and chapped their hands. When alone, they went through a manhood ritual of rolling their trucks or cars into ditches and then enjoyed making offhand comments about those "accidents" in a way we girls could overhear.

I loved going out on Saturday night with Gordon, but at the same time I dreaded it. I couldn't think of anything to say. Gordon said very little also. We did nothing for an hour or more except drive five miles back and forth between the two local restaurants, the Blue Goose and the Red Rooster. So, I rode the familiar route in painful silence, wishing I could say something. Around nine o'clock, Gordon would get some fries with brown gravy and milkshakes at the Blue Goose. We ate in his pickup because only men and women committed to each other appeared in public together.

From the Blue Goose, he drove to a secluded area where we parked and experimented. One pair of hands, guided equally by desire and fear, halfheartedly thwarted the other pair that sought greater intimacy. Although I was attracted to Gordon and liked the excitement of his advances, I never considered a future with him. In addition to the sexual experimentation, I dated because I wanted to do what my peers did. Unbeknownst to me, my two friends understood that dating spelled marriage.

Edith, Della and I spent as much time as we could talking about our guys (not often because they had so many responsibilities). Usually it took place after supper in the 1951 gray Chevy my father gave me that year, when I was thirteen. I wonder if my parents discussed the liabilities of my driving without a license–I couldn't get one until I turned sixteen. I was thankful for the car; I lived too far away to walk to my friends' homes in the evenings when it was dark.

Mostly we didn't drive far, only to the other side of the marsh in front of my house, where no one lived. It gave us privacy to ask pressing questions such as: "Did Gordon open the door for you?" "Did Ray ask what you wanted from the restaurant, or did he just get something?" and "Do you think Barry will come this Saturday?" We talked about the plaid cotton skirts we painstakingly sewed using tissue paper patterns; about using the right amount of starch to stiffen our crinolines and about caring for navy and white saddle shoes.

The Chevy also provided music, our only connection with the world beyond our village. With as much oomph as any teenager anywhere, we sang along with Elvis Presley, Jerry Lee Lewis, Pat Boone, Kitty Wells, Johnny Cash and Hank Williams, among others. We three delighted in it equally and, as such, those musical interludes breached the divides of our backgrounds. How fortunate we were to have the great Elvis Presley; even today, he's a favorite of mine. Looking back, the music was the best part of my adolescent years.

Edith and Della sometimes gossiped for long periods about townspeople whom I didn't know well or care much about. Instead of listening, I paid attention to inner thoughts that repeatedly regretted I didn't have more interesting things to do. This pattern of blocking out what I didn't want to hear intensified in the future, happening not only when I suffered from tedium but also when I was especially anxious. It diminished my self-confidence and social abilities.

During the month of October, rural schools closed for three weeks so older children could pick potatoes, the Island's big crop and, needing to be part of the mainstream as well as wanting some money, I plunged in. I walked to the farm next door where I'd been hired and waited in the hot kitchen dreading someone might say something to me. Shortly there were half a dozen people I either didn't know well or at all; we walked to a field where frost still lay on the ground and breathed in the earthy odor of freshly overturned dirt left in the wake of a tractor uncovering the potatoes.

Stooping over, legs saddling a row of scattered potatoes, we picked, inching our woven bushel baskets along between our feet. Once full, with a heave we hoisted them up and over into a dump cart hauled by a draft horse. In no time my white cotton gloves became caked with dirt, but at least shyness didn't bother me much: I felt only exhaustion. We picked until cold afternoon shadows covered the ground and we could hardly see, to about four-thirty.

When I was fifteen, for four or five nights I slept over at a large potato farm several miles away. I felt adventuresome but spoke little. Though picking potatoes broadened my knowledge of P.E.I., it provoked concerns over what I was doing: working in a field listening to teenagers say nothing that interested me. Worse, they made lewd comments about animals and sex that shocked me. What bothered me most, though, what really hurt, was knowing it was only my lack of self-confidence that kept me from going away to school and being with more compatible peers. I felt powerless.

I finished grade ten in Hampton. The closest high school was in the capital of the Island, Charlottetown, twenty-five miles away. I was only fourteen, and my parents decided I was too young to live away on my own, so I repeated the year. Boring the first time, it got worse and, being the only person in that grade, the teacher paid me scant attention. My two girlfriends were becoming absorbed in their boyfriends, Edith planning to marry Gordon (one summer he started dating her while I was visiting Nana) and Della, Barry. About all I can recall about that year is reading Canadian history more than ever and feeling as if I were in a vacuum.

ꝏ

Modeled after schools in England, my high school was called Prince of Wales College, even though it was just a two-year institution offering grades eleven and twelve. To attend the school, I lived in a small boardinghouse owned by an elderly couple and went home on weekends in my Chevy. My mother found me a roommate, June, the daughter of a friend of hers from a neighboring town. I was continually grateful for her doing that: it was about the only time she helped me with a social situation and I wished she'd help me more. June and I got along well during those two years, although we did different things; I studied and she had a job. Engaged to a farmer who earned very little, she worked as a telephone operator to save some money before they married. Her fiancé's father was one of the three Islanders who committed suicide; he did it so the income from his potato farm would stretch a little further.

In my big new school I joined the top of the streamlined classes and loved the work, especially new-to-me subjects such as physics, chemistry and Latin. I received straight honors, but I had no social life, neither male nor female. I had one girl acquaintance: we walked with each other between classes but barely spoke, and did nothing else together. I still had no idea how to develop a conversation and it appeared she didn't either.

I didn't discover companions through books because other than textbooks, I did not read much. The English Literature teacher baffled me—and I think most of my class—with his lectures. When he read I heard strings of syllables by

Browning, Keats or Burns enunciated with an Irish accent in a voice that went from a whisper to a bellow with no warning. Understanding little, my attention floated from the small English pug lying by his side to his non-matching socks; from his round face to his bulging eyes that became dreamy-looking when he recited certain poems. I don't remember that he assigned any homework.

Although my parents loved to read, I read only books about horses like *Black Beauty* and *Misty* and then only during the three years I rode Jenny. I realize now my parents set an excellent model in their reading habits, but during those middle teenage years, I remained mired in concerns about my shy personality, my future and, what seemed to me, a pretty desolate life.

ꟹ

In the summer months during my high school years, my parents spent hours every afternoon tending to hobbies and interests. They collected antiques and maintained a barely operational schooner in Charlottetown, which I only went to see once. One summer they drove around the Island photographing houses for a pamphlet my mother wrote called, *Prince Edward Island Architecture*, which she self-published under the pen name of Lucy Clayton. I saw that my mother had talent, but I didn't relate to her interests and accomplishments. I didn't have any projects and felt out of it. I think I suffered from despondency, summer not being a fun time to be alone when you're sixteen and seventeen.

By this time, fall of 1959, the eight long winters of isolation my mother had endured starting taking their toll, although, for the most part, she didn't complain. She didn't protest when the furnace failed to warm the house or about being snowbound for several months–she didn't have the strength to walk our long lane covered in deep snow (no one plowed driveways then). She suffered from many illnesses, including depression, severe arthritis, phlebitis and gingivitis. The doctor gave her medications, and when they failed, she consumed a lot of alcohol.

When I was home weekends and on vacations, she invited me to join her, so I began smoking cigarettes and drinking frothy homemade beer. Nowadays, people are more aware of the possible disastrous effects of alcohol on teenagers' brains. But in 1959 I learned that drink alleviated my own tensions, so I kept on using it for that reason for more than twenty years. My father, twelve years older than my mother, seemed oblivious to her habit and my brother was usually away at school. No one noticed the drinking but me, and I didn't know what to make of it, let alone what to say about it.

We drank in the room with the piano she now seldom played, she in her pretty black rocker and I across from her, on the blue velvet antique sofa. With Nat gone, we didn't use the card table for bridge. I kept my drink on it, sometimes wishing I were playing cards. "Always count your blessings," my mother said with a great deal of emphasis on the word ***always***. Usually, I was fairly dutiful and docile, but I didn't know of any blessings to count. I could only think of feeling lonely, of being unable to express myself, of fearing the world was suited for other people, not for me. But, even with my mother, I couldn't say this. I never told anyone my worries. It didn't seem appropriate to complain about something that was going on only in my mind.

During those afternoon talks, I wanted guidance about my future, but instead of helping me, she talked mainly about her childhood–the German nurses, the black servants, the goats, carts, playing with balls. It was so unlike my life, it could have been a fairy tale. It seemed as if she wanted to think about her being a girl, rather than her daughter, her girl, me, sitting in front of her. I felt dreadful. I drank too much.

My mother frequently praised me. "You're so lucky, Helen, you're so young and pretty, and so very smart!" My insides would recoil when she said this. I thought my age seemed a given and my so-called good looks and intelligence were of no use because I didn't talk with anyone or do anything. People now know mixing alcohol with drugs for depression or pain muddles one's thinking, and my mother's state of mind may have influenced her to rationalize that my good looks, youth and intelligence made me capable of organizing my life, thereby relieving her from becoming involved.

Then one afternoon in an offhand manner she said, "Be sure you marry someone with money," with emphasis on the word *money*. For me, marriage seemed such a long way off that the idea of finding a rich husband seemed irrelevant. I only wanted a social life and a plan for the future, not a husband. I wonder now how she felt about her own life and about not having the kind of wealth she grew up with.

Becoming curious, I asked, "Where do you think I'll be married?" "Oh, I always thought right here, in this room," she replied casually. This response mortified me. Did it mean my parents expected me to marry a local person? I didn't dare ask. With considerable horror, I wondered if my parents thought I should stay on the Island because I was so shy–that maybe they thought I was unfit to live anywhere else. I knew I couldn't marry anyone like Gordon, Barry or Ray, guys who had not interested me that way in the least.

Desperately, I searched my inexperienced mind, time and again, about how I would be able to support myself in the future. Using a pencil and a piece of paper, I despaired when I realized I couldn't make a living from selling eggs, the only business I could think of. I didn't consider professions as possibilities, because they would involve people and conversations that frightened me.

As in the past when something overwhelmed me, I tried to forget the issue as much as I could. But that was my life I was ignoring, and it hurt. I chewed my nails to the quick, making them pretty unsightly, especially because I have large hands and long fingers like my mother.

After my parents went to bed, I'd spend many evenings in the kitchen where I studied my class work with my socked feet on the open oven door to keep them warm, a custom I'd observed at my former friends' homes. There they burned wood, not oil like us, and their ovens were cozier.

My father would wake up at around 9:30 and join me, having a bowl of cornflakes. He reminisced about growing up, his role in World War I and his work at Standard Oil. He also gave me advice.

"Don't be persuaded by people to be like them. Decide for yourself what's best for you. Don't let money and what others have influence you." At other times he advised, "Be true to yourself; be kind to others and live simply. You'll always be happy you did." I was too immature to understand much then, but I knew he was trying to be helpful, because the conviction and love in his voice still reverberate in my mind.

His degree of integrity and honesty contrasts with that of many Americans, especially as I write today, in January 2009, with the exposure of inconceivable government and business corruption. My father, always living up to his values while he served as Chief of Shipping at Standard Oil, declined a bribe from a man with an easily recognizable surname seeking preferences for his shipping routes.

Sometimes during our evenings I would ask, "Dad, I don't know what to do now. What am I gonna do?" "Helen, I'm too old to help you, but ideas will come to you. You don't need to worry about it now." But that reply really let me down. I had no one else I felt comfortable with to ask that question and soon I would be done with high school.

True, I had seldom asked my parents' advice about anything, not even about what I should wear or questions about my homework, and my parents hadn't developed the habit of counseling me. Now, when I needed advice, my father was too old and my mother oblivious. Students have guidance counselors today at high schools, but there was no such help at my school.

☙

Visiting Nana exacerbated my sense of alienation on the Island. I loved Nana and staying with her, but at her place I realized I didn't belong in the world of my cousins, either. A few of them attended private schools. Some wore attractive and stylish clothing, saw the latest shows in New York City, attended parties and something called "coming-out parties."

I didn't have a school life or a social one I wanted to discuss and the closest thing I had come to "coming out" consisted of leaving town to pick potatoes.

For a few years some cousins sent me their worn dancing gowns. I would have loved some of their used blue jeans, sweaters or windbreakers—those were the only clothes I wore. Why didn't my mother talk with those cousins about the inappropriateness of sending me dresses? On top of being useless to me, the gowns reminded me of a lifestyle I was missing.

On weekends at home in Hampton, I felt sad, lonely or bored, in no special order. The worst of those times were on awesomely gorgeous, moonlit Saturday nights. Standing in the hallway beside the front door, my nose pressed to a windowpane etched with frost, I saw for miles. I saw snow drifting gently, trees and fences casting curious silhouettes on ghostly fields stretching down to the black and white marsh, and beyond that, red and green Northern Lights glittering over the Northumberland Straits. My elderly parents asleep, I witnessed this beauty alone, feeling dreadfully sorry for myself. In a way, it was as if I were still locked in my childhood room in Cos Cob, only worse. Now I was a young woman, it was Saturday night and I was free, but I had no one to be with.

Sometime during this period when I had so little social life, I left a suicide letter in my top bureau drawer, and I wonder if anyone ever read it.

I did date one boy, toward the end of high school. And although it infuriated me at the time, it was fortunate, as far as my future was concerned, that my parents steadfastly opposed this boyfriend. I had "fallen in love" with Arnold when he and I were both ten, when my mother and I visited his family in Victoria, the fishing village across the marsh in front of our house. I hadn't seen him in seven years, but when he came calling one night, his cute smile, sparkling dark brown eyes and wavy brown black hair roused my old feelings for him. He didn't have a car, though, so I rarely saw him.

Arnold and his friends had a reputation in town for being "wild"—they sped late at night on the highway, presumably drinking. Rumor in town circulated that sometimes Arnold rode on top of the car, holding on to a rope, much as I'd held on to reins while standing on a fast-moving wood sleigh in order to feel alive and exhilarated.

Although desperate to have the world make sense for us, Arnold and I couldn't verbalize our anxieties. When we dated we just rode around in the back of a friend's car while the others talked in front. But looking into his eyes, an electric current subdued my worries. Our kisses relaxed me and freed me from loneliness.

My parents forbade me to see him. I got mad. "He's the only person I've got to see and I want to see him." My father got mad. "I forbid you to ever see him again and don't ever talk about it!" I became sulky and negative. I knew that Arnold wasn't good for me, but I couldn't tolerate being alone any longer. Without telling anyone, I decided if I had to live on P.E.I., I'd marry him and let the future play out as it might.

Then in a few days Arnold dropped off a bag of live lobsters at our house, and the second he left, my father stuffed them in the garbage can under the sink. Like never before, a raging voice bellowed up from deep inside and at a substantial pitch I yelled, "My God, this place is so boring! Why are we living here? I hate it! There's nothing for me to do here!"

No one answered my question. I looked around. No one but I was still downstairs. This outburst could have been an opportunity to discuss my future, but my family denied emotions, so they didn't stay with me when I cried out. I felt drained and just a little delirious from having shouted my suffering, but not for long. In the next minute reality slammed me in the face. I saw no relief, no exit strategy, no one to help me find a better life.

But my mother must have written about my outburst to Nana, because she offered to send me abroad. In a couple of weeks my cousin Beth was leaving on a summer-long voyage to Italy on a private tour, consisting of an adult guide and five girls, all seventeen like me. An uncle who worked in the shipping business could secure a berth. I was ecstatic!

My grandmother left her summer home in Maine for New York just to buy me some clothes and see me off. Having visited the Island, she knew I never wore anything but inexpensive, plain clothing. We spent three days at Saks, Lord and Taylor's and B. Altman where she made sure I got everything I needed. And she waited hours while I selected three evening dresses, my first ever.

ௐ

At sea, on board the glorious old Italian liner the *Augustus*, my world became splendid. There was so much to see, starting with the beautiful well-polished wood of the vessel itself. The ship was small enough to walk everywhere aside from the first-class area which, for us, was out of bounds. However, someone invited us seventeen-year-olds up there for dances. I danced for the first time. I was ecstatic.

Beth busied herself with getting to know the other girls on our tour who, like her, attended private schools. From the Main Line, when I'd seen her in Kennebunk I noticed she tended to wear stylish clothing and real gold jewelry. I'd often felt inconsequential around her.

Now I presumed that not just she but also the other tour members considered me to be quiet and uninteresting, from an unheard-of place. At first I found it hard to be largely ignored by my group, but soon the wonders of being at sea with hundreds of eclectic people lifted my spirits and I ignored my group's stand-off behavior.

The ocean itself mesmerized me for hours. Sometimes I stared at our white wake churning endlessly way into the wide blue expanse, and at night I watched moonbeams dance on gigantic, textured billows of dark water undulating in a soothing, up-down motion. My mind relaxed and swayed with the movement.

Soon I met an attractive fellow, my age, from New York City, traveling with his parents. We remained casual friends for the duration of the voyage, talking about New York and what we saw and did on the ship. P.E.I. stayed out of my thoughts.

I'd never spoken with a well-educated, attentive male and loved it. When we disembarked in Venice, my group went on a gondola ride, and my leader and my friend's parents arranged for us to ride in the same boat before our paths diverged.

After spending a week viewing paintings, sculpture and the watery wonders of Venice and then another one seeing art treasures in Florence, we piled into a van and zigzagged along the Amalfi Drive high above the Mediterranean, all the while my emotions soaring to an unfamiliar zenith with excitement. Then we entered Rome, the city whose name for me conjured the epitome of the word *civilization*, and I felt even more sublime.

For me the ruins of Rome had been words and pictures, until one day at the Coliseum, in the palm of my hand I held rubble from the Empire, the Republic and the present. I saw the whole world come together, two periods from the past and the present. In an instant I was moved by this insight into history. I realized that circumstances change, but the permanence of our struggles does not. Although this didn't make me feel better about my personal life, by understanding such a universal concept, my self-confidence received a boost.

We stayed in the fabled city for six weeks at a former palace. The bedroom I shared with three others on the tour was as large as a stately ballroom. During cocktails in the living room, our tour leader introduced us to Ettore, a bachelor and a baron who lived in the "palace" while he studied for a postgraduate degree in architectural engineering.

He was a few years older, quiet, with blue eyes and pale skin, slender and just a little taller than I. Although he dressed smartly, as did many Italians I saw, he didn't exude the kind of ardor for women that some men did, ones who, upon introduction, might kiss you from your hand up to your elbow.

After dinner, Ettore sat with our group and I got to know him, though his English was quite limited. I think he liked my quiet and straightforward manner, and that I didn't try to impress him or ply him with questions in an attempt to show an interest in him, as I watched the other girls do. He had a sweet smile, as others have said about me.

We liked each other pretty quickly, in a romantic way, too. He took me to exclusive nightclubs–including an outdoor one beside the Tivoli Fountain where light from dozens of tiny electric bulbs bounced on the shadowy water. When dancing, Ettore guided me in such a way that I relaxed, and I felt especially wonderful when they played our standard request, "Summer Love." We didn't try the more difficult Latin numbers.

I felt attractive in the evening dresses Nana had bought me: they looked as stylish as anything I saw others wearing. One strapless fitted gown with muted black and white squares had a cute short jacket I removed for dancing, and another white dress with a fitted top and full skirt had yellow trim and pretty, matching embroidered shoulder straps.

Often, Ettore liked to look at me and tell me I was pretty. But after I had a complete hair and facial makeover done by professionals at Max Factor's headquarters, his eyes never left me all evening. My hairstyle gave shape and volume to my small head; eyeliner and eye shadow gave prominence to my eyes, and together with powders and lipstick, I might have been an actress. Even strangers stared. The constant attention bothered me, and the next day I was glad to look like my regular self again, although I continued to use a few of Max Factor's applications when I went out with Ettore.

Before he took me home in his Fiat each night, we embraced and he showered me tenderly with kisses for a few minutes. There were no awkward moments because he didn't try anything beyond that. We didn't speak each other's language, which was perfect for me, as I wasn't expected to say much.

My five tour mates strove to resemble models in *Seventeen* magazine and wanted dates, but they hardly had any and, I believed, were puzzled over mine. Some became guardedly respectful—one even invited me to the ice-cream parlor a few times. At first she plied me with questions about my background, but when I ignored them, she talked about other things. I sensed she and I learned there are different types of charm and it helped me to realize I needn't be talkative in order to be liked.

Why did I receive so much attention from men? I've read some guys prefer to be with shy women and none of the other girls appeared shy. Today, I can see that in my silence, I may have appeared alluringly mysterious. In addition, the guys were mostly quite young and not too experienced, and I may have been the most approachable. And, as for me, perhaps because the trip was so exhilarating, so unbelievably exciting, I might have radiated a joy that was irresistible and contagious.

This leaves me now with the question, what is shyness and why wasn't I shy on the voyage?

At different times, I was. I was bashful, timid and self-conscious on the ship, but only during some brief moments. Chronic shyness is so much more than that. It's a persistent emotional condition, one I normally couldn't shake off in Cos Cob and P.E.I. and for much of my life. Today I believe my shy disposition wouldn't have made me feel so uncomfortable unless other influences—negative ones—fueled it. In other words, the degree of discomfort I felt from shyness varied in proportion to the degree of adverse conditions affecting my well-being.

And when I stepped off the liner in New York and watched my tour mates dash with open arms to greet friends and family, a miserable gripping fear tore through me from head to toe as I remembered that I had no friends, no demonstrative family, no exciting life. Inferiority struck; I became the old me. An uncle I barely knew put me on a plane for P.E.I. where I had no peers to relive or re-create the trip's experiences. My tour mates hadn't mentioned writing to me and, of course, I wouldn't have thought to initiate that idea myself.

Ettore wrote a few beautiful letters in English, with a gorgeous penmanship I later recognized as typical of architects, about how he'd enjoyed our relationship and about his activities. After I wrote to him he said, "I knew you'd be intelligent, and your letters prove it." (He hadn't learned much about me while we dated because we couldn't talk to each other.) But after a couple of weeks of little to do but stare at empty fields in front of our house, I became depressed and, not wanting to pretend I felt fine or to describe my desultory life, I stopped writing to him.

ଔ

After Italy, I no longer considered Arnold an option. The Island seemed tenfold more boring and unbearable than ever. I was desperate to have friends and things to do, but too afraid to go anywhere on my own.

Then on September 1, 1960, Nat made a rare, short visit home on his way from summer school in Mexico to Dalhousie University. During this visit, we wound up going for a drive with our parents, something we'd seldom done. Sitting in the backseat, a few miles from home, Nat turned toward me. "Where are you going to university?" "I'm not. I don't have any plans." "You gotta go. Everyone does. You have to find one." I was surprised and happy to have someone talk about my future.

As soon as I got home I called Dalhousie and was turned down because their dorms were full. Nat said to try the University of New Brunswick. When I replied to the admission officer's inquiry about my grades at Prince of Wales College, he accepted me over the phone. I had to be there in three days.

I was ready: my need to get away blindsided my shyness, making me temporarily fearless; besides, I was leaving the Island for a known destination and I knew I could handle that. My mother said she'd miss me. In hindsight, especially as a mother, I realize she must have missed me a lot.

The hardest part of writing this memoir has been trying to understand my mother. When speaking with my Jungian analyst about her, he referred to her as a "mystery woman," which caused me to try hard to remember things about her. I recalled more clearly her incessant limping in P.E.I. and agonized grimace. Walking clearly had been painful for her. At the time, I hadn't thought much of it: it seemed an integral part of who she was. Later in life I understood, to some degree, what she may have felt, when I had my own problems with pain. But I was fortunate to benefit from what scientists discovered in the last few decades to control pain and to have found a great neurosurgeon who instructed me how to manage it. But with my mother's pain, I can see it may have been difficult for her to be more in the moment, to be more with me and my problems.

Now I also realize just how different I was from my mother, so different that she may not even have been aware of my unhappiness. I was quiet, pensive and inward-looking. She liked gardening, making crafts, doing things. We shared a love for music, but in P.E.I. she played with less verve than in Cos Cob and her classical records sounded tinny on our inexpensive record player.

She may have had acute anxiety problems of her own, not the least of which may have resulted from her sister, at around age thirty-five, being transported to a mental institution where she remained confined for six years. My mother never spoke about this part of her sister's life, or about any other important personal worries—at least not in a way that invited help. Rather, she accepted problems. To accept life and its difficulties appears to have been the way women of her social environment were brought up, and some of them suffered from it all their lives.

Perhaps she didn't want to discuss my problems because of her grin-and-bear-it attitude, choosing instead to focus on the positive, by telling me how lucky I was to be so smart and pretty. I understand my mother a little better today, but I still can't condone my parents' decision to move to P.E.I. When parents have a choice, they tend to move to an area that offers promise for their children. Why didn't mine? I can only speculate that it resulted from my father's wish to be as far away as he could from the turmoil of city life, to be able to enjoy living simply. They didn't realize that the social conditions would trouble Nat and me.

I never asked them why they moved there. Maybe it just wasn't in my nature yet to ask "why" questions. Perhaps I'd learned from my mother to "accept."

As troublesome as it was for us, Nat and I were never callous about our parents' peculiar decision to live on P.E.I., or about their being too old to be more helpful. Yes, they made an outlandish decision to move, but they were equally unusual and brave to have children so late in life and, if it hadn't been for that, we wouldn't have been born.

5

1960–1964: Anchors Aweigh!

On September 6, 1960, my father drove me to the Saint John River Valley and on up the wide river to Fredericton and the University of New Brunswick (U.N.B.). I began to feel afraid and cried. My father said, "Don't worry, Helen. Wait. You'll see–everything will turn out fine."

After leaving my luggage in the dorm, my father came with me to the registration building, wished me well and said goodbye. I looked inside the large auditorium and saw long, straggly lines of students, people who looked like me, shuffling quietly through masses of paper. *Good, maybe I can fit in.* I'd given no thought to careers and didn't know I'd have to select a major the day I registered. I spent little time thinking about it though–I chose history, the story of humankind, which Aunt Llewellyn had taught me to appreciate. My main concerns that day were not about studies, but about what to say to people.

After returning from registering, I met my two roommates. One came from a small town north of Fredericton. I said hello and she said, "I can't talk much with you or with anyone. I've got to use every bit of my time studying to keep my scholarship." I turned away quickly, not wanting to waste more of her time. Although I didn't know what to expect from students, it appeared she couldn't be friendly and I wished she wasn't my roommate.

The other roommate, a black woman from Jamaica, seemed older. I watched her walk in a slow, rhythmic way, holding her head more erect than anyone I'd ever seen. She ate at the Dean of Women's table, and spent the rest of her time going between classes and the library. In hindsight, I see she must have been dealing with being the only black woman on campus. It didn't occur to me that her experience with racism might have caused her to stay apart and seek safe harbor with the dean. At the time I thought she felt superior.

I had no preparation for university, except my father had told me the most important thing a person could learn there was critical thinking. That hadn't meant a lot to me, and in my naïveté, it didn't sound difficult. I liked U.N.B. for its small population, about fifteen hundred people; for its diverse faculties—forestry, liberal arts, sciences, engineering and nursing; for its casualness and because its anthem was sung to Sousa's "Anchors Aweigh," the U.S. Navy march my mother frequently played. When I heard it at U.N.B., it both grounded me and set me free.

Although my two roommates didn't fulfill any of my social needs, a girl at the other end of the hallway did. Unique to U.N.B., Willa clamored for attention and friends. With big jowls, puffy lips, sparkling blue circular eyes and jet-black hair arranged alluringly around her cute pale face, Willa came from a culturally savvy life in Ontario. She charmed a small group of us right away by saying, "There's an initiation dance coming up, girls, and we want to be invited!"

In a way, it was Willa who taught me how a shy person could get by. When she introduced me, she'd say I'd been to Italy the previous summer, thereby giving me some status—no doubt to suit her needs more than mine. Reference to my trip got me into discussions, but it also suited my shy inclination to avoid being more personal.

As a result, rather than ask people about their lives, to find ways to join them in doing something, we talked about traveling. I was self-conscious and not good at observing people then, and as a consequence didn't discover how others arranged to get together, to make friends. I didn't learn at university, or for years afterward, that you get to do things with peers by talking about common interests. As a consequence of not doing that, I wound up doing most things by myself. That drawback didn't affect my dating: I relied on men to do the inviting.

Willa was one of a few dozen students in Liberal Arts who came from universities in Ontario and Quebec to do make-up work at U.N.B. because its academic standards were lower. Culturally more colorful than many Maritimers, these students formed a group in the cafeteria, which I joined, thanks to her. I met Peter there, a Liberal Arts student from Montreal. Bilingual, tall and distinguished-looking, he spoke comfortably with the others about cultural happenings in Montreal and Toronto.

He and I began to meet every day and, after coffee, he usually walked me home, comforting me by leaning his frame sideways over my head and placing a firm hand my shoulders. En route to my dorm one day he queried in his fuzzy soft voice, "I want to be like a big brother, like a protector. Is that okay with you?" "Yeah," I said out loud. *Oh how wonderful! Yes, I sure do want a friend and you're perfect.*

Though I felt relaxed with Peter, it didn't seem appropriate to tell him my worries, such as feeling frightened in social situations. He didn't reveal any personal thoughts to me. Eventually I learned he liked a male engineering student who frequently sat near us in the cafeteria. I was shocked to know my friend liked a man, but I decided what mattered most was having someone to care for me, even though I now knew we could never be more than friends of a casual sort. I can see today that this relationship suited me because I wouldn't have any emotional involvements to deal with.

I learned to appreciate classical music with Peter in the University's Music Hut, a one-room white wooden building that looked like a shed for storing tools. Stocked with records, we usually had the place to ourselves. One day, wrapped in the comfort of his arms, a Rachmaninoff piano concerto lulled me into a quasi-hypnotic state of aesthetic appreciation. Tears trickled down my face. Peter pushed back some of my hair that had fallen on my face. "It's so good you're crying, Helen. It shows you're experiencing the music deeply, as it should be. Hey. Now you're initiated to classical music. Congratulations!" I felt so warm and loved. I recognized the joy my mother must have with her music, and it felt good to have something in common with her.

Sometimes Peter and the others in our group bantered about witticisms and jokes from books they seemed to be familiar with but I'd never heard of, such as *Winnie the Pooh*. When they laughed and quoted something exotic such as:

"Piglet sidled up to Pooh from behind. 'Pooh,' he whispered. 'Yes, Piglet?' 'Nothing,' said Piglet, taking Pooh's paw, 'I just wanted to be sure of you,"' I cringed because I didn't want anyone to know how little I'd read.

It wasn't until recently that a writer friend told me *Winnie the Pooh* was usually read to children. With a fleeting ache, I acknowledged I couldn't recall having been read to by my parents, although I could fondly remember Nana reading *Uncle Wiggily* to me at her hotel.

And so at these difficult moments, I would glance downward, half smile and kind of pretend to understand what the group was laughing about. I liked these people, though; they seemed open-minded, nonjudgmental and other than when they alluded to unknown-to-me literary characters, I felt comfortable with them.

But then there was the day when Peter wasn't in the cafeteria, and a group regular, a doctoral student in psychology, looked me straight in the eyes from the other end of the table. "Helen, what's wrong with you! You're the quietest person I've ever seen. Can't you talk? Don't you ever have anything you want to say?"

Gaping at him, I muttered as low as I could, "I'm okay." *Yes, Gary, there are things I'd like to say all the time and would if I could. Do you have to be so rude?* I left shortly, studying my feet and holding back tears, cursing him under my breath and at the same time damming myself for being unable to speak.

ൠ

Sometimes I missed the evening curfew by just a minute or two—never intentionally—but because I hated to lose a second with Peter and the group and at the cafeteria. The Dean scowled at me more than once, "Why can't you get back on time!" I despised the little check-in room and the huge clock on the wall with its long black hands, and the more the Dean complained the more I was late. As a solution, Peter told me he knew of a woman, Mary Jean, who had an apartment and wanted a roommate. I contacted her and in January of 1961, became the first woman student at U.N.B. to obtain permission to live on her own.

Mary Jean seemed to be a private person, accustomed to comfort. Well-spoken with a cute laugh, her appearance and apartment reflected a lackadaisical manner, though I suspected it was somewhat contrived. I assumed she'd graduated a few years earlier from U.N.B., but she spoke little about herself, and since I wasn't one to garner or share information, I never found out for sure. About all we did together was clean the apartment and shop for food and large quantities of spirits.

Mary Jean stocked a two-tiered bar on wheels. Two or three Hungarian post-doctoral students, friends of hers, visited a couple of times a week to talk and drink late into the night. I liked to hear their down-to-earth chatter about their studies and about the fighting that ravished their country in 1956.

But then trouble arrived one day in February, when I was sick in bed. Peter stopped by. I looked and felt so terrible that I didn't get up, but from my bed I overheard Mary Jean lashing out: "What are you doing, Peter! You're coming here all the time to see Helen–it's too much. She's got to study; you know that. You're being dreadfully inconsiderate of her needs! For heaven's sake, leave her alone so she can get some work done!" Then I heard him thumping down the stairs.

Her scolding must have shocked and angered Peter a great deal because he refused to speak with me again. I was too shy to vent my anger to Mary Jean for lambasting my friend and not brave enough to speak with Peter, to tell him I'd had nothing to do with it. I despaired over how little control I exercised over my life, how it hurt that others ran it, that I was too weak to intervene. And now I hated to walk around campus because when I saw Peter–who soon had a new woman friend–he ignored me.

Not wanting to be reminded of my loss, I avoided anyplace I thought Peter might be, especially the cafeteria. So instead of having several friendly faces to greet there every day, I had only one social contact, Mary Jean, at home, whom I silently blamed for changing my life. For me University was a place to learn to be with people and I was failing. I didn't turn to my studies for an escape. I hadn't yet learned to stimulate my mind with knowledge, with ideas from homework; also, I didn't find it necessary to study. By using what I'd learned at high school combined with paying attention in lectures, I was able to pass everything at mid-term. I wrote essays that I knew were way under-researched, and yet I got by with them, too. Now, instead of socializing or studying, I shuffled from class to class to home, with a pounding emotional ache.

I went to P.E.I. for Easter. Going back to U.N.B., the ferry took four extra hours breaking thick ice in its path. And in Fredericton, I opened the door to a colder than usual apartment. There was no note, but I gathered from Mary Jean's empty closet that she'd left. She called to say little except she wasn't returning. I heard weeks later she had a baby.

I realize I knew little at that time about emotions–either good ones or bad ones. Eventually a whole new school of therapy revealed the importance of recognizing feelings, but it didn't exist then. I had no one to speak with and I had no direction or zest for any pursuit. Alone and lonely, I reverted to the only way I knew to feel better–drinking–and many days after classes, I drank from Mary's Jean's former big bar into oblivion.

One night the doctoral student in psychology, the one who'd criticized me for being so quiet, saw my light on and–I've no idea how he knew anything about my personal life–dropped in to lecture me. "You have responsibilities to your parents who sent you here to study. You're just wasting their money; you're not even trying to pass, and you'll fail. It's a serious matter for your university record if that happens, and worse, you'd have to do the whole year over."

To my way of thinking my parents didn't really send me–I'd asked to go. But it now occurred that maybe my parents wouldn't want to pay for me to come back if I failed, and that really scared me...returning to the Island would be intolerable. Then, in addition, I realized I wouldn't want to fail anything anyway and I nodded, "Thanks Gary, I'll work on it."

I appreciated his concern and started to follow his advice. I studied hard, sometimes even with gusto. I passed everything except English. I couldn't understand how to write essays for it; the questions posed dealt with elements of technique and style, topics I couldn't even define. I consulted with my English professor. I may have been too shy or didn't know how to explain that I didn't understand the essay questions, but he didn't help. However, that failure was good because it took me off the Island that summer to take the make-up course.

At home for six weeks before the summer session began, I now had something to do: examine my English textbook. I studied most of the time, and concentrated on some interesting literature, such as Chaucer's *Canterbury Tales* and Milton's *Paradise Lost*. I found whole scenarios of uniquely peopled worlds, and most of them, I learned, came from the authors' imaginations, through something new to me, called "creativity." I saw the world in a more complex way, maybe in some ways even a wonderful one, but then it was time to go to summer school, so I closed my text and started thinking about the real people I had to interact with.

Willa was my roommate for the summer, although she kept so busy with a handsome curly blond guy that I barely saw her. At first I studied, but I didn't know how to spend time alone and old feelings of despair returned. So, instead of building on what I'd discovered while studying at home, I reverted to doing things I really didn't enjoy in order to avoid loneliness.

I spent many evenings talking in my apartment with a psychology graduate student who sought my company simply because his fiancée was away. My shyness held me back from talking about myself so I didn't benefit from any commentary or insight he might have provided had I told him my problems. One good thing came of these evenings, however:

toward the end of the summer, a friend of this man's, Nancy, came by to see if she could room with me the following year. (I was still one of the few women living on my own.) Large-framed with a lovable smile, her beautiful high-pitched voice hung in the air after she stopped talking. I thought she was great.

After summer school and a typical quiet few days at home, I returned in the fall of 1961 with enthusiasm, only to learn my new roommate spent much of her time at the library, leaving me on my own. However, through her I met Jimmy, a third-year political science student with whom Nancy had gone to high school.

ᘛ

Jimmy saw Nancy and me together somewhere and, after asking her about me, he just came by, flashed his cute mischievous smile and wooed me in an instant. Slender, about five-eight or a couple of inches taller than I, like me he wasn't at all athletic, although he walked with a long, loose stride, especially when it was freezing cold. He had short, wavy dark hair, a narrow freckled face, and a solid nose.

It had been more than six months since I'd had a close friend, and Jimmy helped me relax. He entertained me with stories. Grinning wide enough to expose his yellowish teeth, he joked about the number of books on political science he'd borrowed from the library. With his voice at a high crescendo, he finished the story, "They had to send a truck to my house to pick them up and it was almost full before they left!"

Jimmy would come and stay for two or three nights. He would just stop in, sit down and put his feet up on the coffee table as if he hadn't been away. He didn't ask questions about my personal life and I stuck to my timid habit of going along with the tenor set by the other person.

We shared the warmth of our bodies curled around each other in bed, but we had little physical closeness beyond that. It was fine with me, since I wasn't as physically attracted to him as I'd been to other men and our lack of sexual activity didn't matter.

When I did feel a strong physical attraction for someone and was emboldened by drinking, scenarios of sexual activity created embarrassment, bewilderment and consequential silence, a combination that ended the relationships in no time. Today I suspect my mind acted to protect me from emotions I couldn't handle, and of course I was too shy to discuss these feelings with anyone.

So sex, that bewildering intimacy no one had explained to me in a straightforward fashion and about which I could speak to no one, created such a morass of confusion that it became another source for feeling inferior, compounding my shyness. And, naturally, it strained my dating.

Jimmy and I were honest and loving with each other and that was what mattered. He was with me at the time J.F.K. was assassinated and it was especially good to have a friend then when the whole world was so terribly immersed in fear. Although I'd developed almost no knowledge or interest in politics, it scared me that a sniper could shoot the U.S. president. Between being with Jimmy and studying when he was away, I had a busy year without many unpleasant consequences from shyness.

The only misgiving I had about our relationship was our failure to go out and get to know people, because in April, when he left to study at McGill, I had no one to talk with–a condition that lasted to the end of the year. I reverted to drinking in the evenings.

ര

A year before Nat would have completed a degree in economics at Dalhousie University, he went to live in Madrid. That summer of 1962, after my second year at U.N.B., having decided to minor in Spanish, I asked my parents if I could visit him for a few weeks to practice the language and they agreed.

Nat and his Spanish girlfriend, Angela, ten years older than he, met me at the airport and with their help I soon became familiar with the colorful and dynamic plaza called La Puerta del Sol, the center of the country's capital. We stayed one block from Puerta del Sol, in a four-story hostel called La Marlasca.

Sometimes Angela and I went out for coffee. I can still picture her sipping double expressos with her large, nervous brown eyes rolling around while she described in rapid broken English her survival in Madrid during the Spanish Civil War, 1936–39.

"I lived with my aunt because my parents died in a car accident. We almost starved to death. We had no food. People were shooting in the streets and we had to stay indoors, and when it became dark we got scared. We had nothing to eat. Sometimes all we had were bugs we caught in the building. I prayed all the time for the shooting to stop." It was hard for me to respond verbally to her suffering, but my heart went out to her.

Angela made me feel less shy, as did other Spanish-speaking people. Spaniards seemed to revel in emotions, smiling grandly, gesturing with their arms and modulating the volume of their voices. When I was with Angela, my emotions squirmed to get out, begging to be acknowledged; with her I smiled more and displayed more feelings than I normally did. I noticed that about Nat, too. I fell in love with the ambiance of Madrid and thought what a perfect decision my brother had made to live there.

I felt more relaxed in Spain than in North America owing to a somewhat convoluted misconception. I believed it was customary for people to talk with one another when they shared the same space, and being too shy to do that, I would feel self-conscious and inferior. Today I see it is quite normal and polite either to talk or not talk when with others. However, in Spain I didn't have this problem. I thought people would believe I was being quiet simply because I didn't speak their language.

Feeling as free as I did while braving blizzards on the Island, I explored the noisy streets filled with little cars and peculiar, smelly fumes, watching pedestrians communicate with endless, demonstrative gestures. *How can they talk so freely?! Don't they ever feel self-conscious? I can't believe it...they laugh from their stomachs. I never saw anyone in my family do that, or anyone on the Island. And the way they flash their black-brown eyes, even at me, without knowing me. They're never shy. They speak right up with whatever's on their mind. What if I'd been born here! If only, if only! I could never have turned out shy. I'd be a totally different person. Darn the stiff and stuffy English culture that I'm descended from.*

At least once every day I went to one of the huge old cafe salons, where I drank hot chocolate or espresso and ate a delicious pastry, each one with an imaginative name, such as Elephant Ears. On languid afternoons, I stayed in my hotel room and learned more about Spaniards from reading the books Nat lent me by Hemingway or by turn-of-the-century Spanish authors such as Pio Baroja. They made North American culture pale compared with their two thousand years of diverse civilizations. It made me ponder my uncomfortable background. *I'm neither Canadian or American. What am I?*

ꝏ

The next summer I enrolled in a course on medieval Eastern European History because someone had said the professor was good and in one on American Literature because I wanted to learn about my birth country. However, as was my custom, I didn't study much, being preoccupied with trying to find people to talk with so I wouldn't be lonely.

One day I took a deck of cards to the cafeteria and soon got a game of bridge going. I did well at it and reflected a healthy confidence while playing. It was wonderful, blissful, to do something without feeling self-conscious. In one game, I met Gerry, a psychology major at Dalhousie. She joked and laughed and talked herself into my life, providing the straight-on approach I needed because I didn't speak with ease without encouragement.

Gerry had more spirit and gusto than anyone I'd ever met. She seemed to have the world in her hands: she sang, played the guitar and "went steady" with the star football player at Dalhousie. When I was with her, much of my shyness evaporated, but not the part that prevented me from talking about my painful side. She kept me so busy I had little time to mope about weaknesses. We swam at the nearby pond, played bridge at the cafeteria, and sometimes drank cheap sherry. I felt elated to have such an outgoing, devoted friend.

One day out of the clear blue sky, she said quite seriously, "You're the sanest person I've ever known!" At first I couldn't believe her and thought she must be kidding, but I noticed she wore a serious expression and I remembered she studied psychology. I'd never spoken to her about my childhood, my inadequacies, my self-consciousness. I'd assumed my demeanor revealed me, as if I wore my self-deprecating thoughts on my forehead. And so this statement of hers meant a great deal to me. Gerry saw a part of me that was strong and purposeful–if only I could find it for myself.

We corresponded while she studied at Dalhousie for the school year. But the next spring when we were both at U.N.B., she didn't call. I was confused. When I bumped into her, I could see warmth in her eyes, but for some reason, she wasn't behaving as a friend.

A couple of months later she wrote a letter that began like this, "I'm ecstatic. I never knew how beautiful and loving God was, He who created our world. I'm so happy to be able to serve Him at the Montreal Convent of the Sacred Heart." It stunned me–I'd no idea she was thinking of becoming a nun. All her letters from then on concentrated on the glory of God; I felt sorry to be on the fringes of her life, to lose my wonderful and only friend. I partially consoled myself by envisioning her contagious enthusiasm cheering up nuns throughout the convent.

Apart from Gerry's friendship, nothing again approximated the sheer joy and excitement of Willa's charisma, Peter's charm and the student lounge coffee group. After three years at university I still remained ill at ease with people. I recall about twenty sort-of friends and many things we did together, but too often I felt awkward.

What could have been "learning" sessions for me—discovering how to talk with others about them or about me—didn't happen. With women acquaintances, I just plain didn't know what to talk about. I questioned the appropriateness of what to say so much that I probably lost the ability to talk naturally. Being aware of this depressed me too, isolating me even more. And perhaps by pushing myself to talk, I appeared too direct, too personal, even needy, thereby frightening people away.

In my fourth year a new problem exacerbated my sense of inferiority: privileged people with elaborate lifestyles. I envied them. My inner voice went on and on about my perceived inferiority and made me so tongue-tied it established a solid barrier right from the start.

Before Nancy graduated and left town, she introduced me to Carol, who was looking for a place to stay. Whereas my friend Gerry had just entered a convent, Carol had left one a few years earlier. Since then, she'd graduated in accounting at U.N.B., the first woman to do so, and now worked downtown as an accountant.

About my height, slender, with blue eyes and short light hair, Carol resembled me in some ways. But unlike me, she was socially adept and, being an avid reader, had formed ideas about the world. I didn't consider her a friend, because if someone didn't declare themselves one, I presumed they weren't. Then just before Christmas, she moved to her parents' home in Moncton to be with her two-year-old daughter. Until then, I hadn't known she had one.

When I saw her years later, she surprised me again. We corresponded about once a year, and when she lived in Edmonton, Alberta, and I in Calgary, she visited me and my husband and our baby Anthony. She hugged me, saying, "Hello, at long last! I'm so glad to see you. When you come to Edmonton, you'll meet my baby, Tony... I named him after Anthony." *Oh my God. Carol is a real friend and I didn't know it. Oh, my God I can't believe she named her son after mine. When will I understand people? When will I feel good with them? I'll just act natural and return the friendship.*

While we'd been roommates, Carol spoke fondly about her courses at U.N.B. and about her professors, especially if we'd had the same ones. Partly as a result of that, and partly because when she left at Christmas and I had no one to talk to for the remainder of the year, I studied seriously for the first time, even in the library. I was rewarded with almost straight A's. My courses fascinated me so much that I began to regret I hadn't learned to appreciate knowledge and ideas sooner.

In Spanish Literature, I was the only student. I sat in the professor's office for the lectures and enjoyed being able to ask all the questions I wanted. I couldn't avoid the homework.

Blood Wedding by Federico Garcia Lorca dealt with the bleak lives of spinsters forced to spend decades serving their widowed mothers. Their hardships underscored that I should be doing more with my life: here I was free, but I couldn't figure out how to take advantage of it.

An anthropology course on several African tribes inspired me to compare my culture with theirs. In one, women gathered firewood all day and men hunted with bows and arrows away from home for weeks. All their customs mesmerized me, but I especially focused on their important rituals to launch adolescents into adulthood. No one had ever shown me how to get there or what it meant to be an adult.

I still loved history. Putting together ideas and facts that made past civilizations make sense and come alive not only came naturally but with joy. Now in my fourth year of University, I could understand the history of humankind, but I could not fathom my own life, and I did not know how to reach out for guidance to plan a career. Jobs still frightened me, because I still had few social skills. And scarier, having a job meant establishing a home of my own in some strange place. *How can I go somewhere without knowing anyone? It's bad enough being alone at school where I feel at home; I'd die of loneliness in a strange city, but I have to try. I have to do something. I'll apply for that job at the library in Toronto.*

I was one of just two students being interviewed on-campus for the position. I had good grades and the right academic background. I pictured myself at work, side by side with fascinating people, enjoying endless learning opportunities, in a modern building situated on a beautiful urban square. But after work I imagined arriving home to emptiness: a dim, plain basement apartment where isolation, loneliness and the inability to meet people swallowed me up.

Arriving for the interview, dread and nervousness from being alone in Toronto won over the allure of the job. I deliberately asked if I could have a cigarette, knowing full well you could smoke almost anywhere in 1964, but not at interviews and never at libraries. Making that request guaranteed I wouldn't be hired and have to face being on my own. With a slight stare and shake of her head, the interviewer methodically began asking questions both she and I knew were a waste of time.

After nights of drinking and fretting over my future, followed by a calamitous graduation with no family present, I could think of nothing to do except return home to the village I disliked so much. I was at a loss. I didn't know life needed hard work to feel good in it. Instead I thought I was a misfit when I felt miserable. Maybe someone had told me once that life required an effort, but I didn't hear it because I'd been too distracted by my emotional discomforts.

I could hardly believe I was back living with my parents again. They'd wintered in Mexico from the time I'd gone to U.N.B. We no longer had animals; my father had given Jenny to a farmer who lived a few miles away. I didn't miss her, but I wondered how she fared and if she ever thought of me, like in the stories I'd read about abandoned horses reminiscing over their former owners. I had no friends and nowhere to visit.

For the upcoming winter, my parents prepared to go to Spain, to be near Nat. Seeing me with nothing to do, they invited me along and I agreed. When we discussed how I would pay for my expenses, my father said, "Don't worry, we'll always provide you with enough to cover your necessities." It felt so strange for my parents to give me money to get by on and yet not help plan my life.

In many ways I was eager to revisit the warm-blooded, demonstrative Spaniards. I didn't feel as shy or inferior with the Spanish as I did with English-speaking people. However, I never forgot for a day during what was to be a four-year sojourn in Spain that being there was the result of a cop-out, a fear, caused by an inability to face life by myself in my native land.

Challenges: Becoming an Adult

6

Kennebunk, Maine

As the jet engines roared in reverse, the captain announced over the P.A.: "It's four-forty-five in Boston and fifty-two degrees with light rain." Fifteen years later, in 1978, I was moving from Portugal to live in Maine.

My cousin Mary, mother of Beth, with whom as a teenager I'd toured Italy, met me in the luggage area. We loaded my seven crates into the ancient dark green pickup that had belonged to our Aunt Llewellyn. I hadn't communicated with Mary for years except for a brief phone call to ask if I could stay with her while I settled into my house.

"I'm sorry about your mother's death. It must be hard for you. Are you tired?" she asked while I climbed into the cab.

"It's late my time, after midnight, but I'm not too tired. Thanks for picking me up and letting me stay with you. After two years of Portugal, it's good to be back."

"Why were you there so long?"

"The kids and I left Calgary to visit for a month, but just a week after we got there, Dad came down with Guillain-

Barré syndrome and from one day to the next he couldn't move...at all." I stopped to regain my composure. "The doctor didn't know what it was for a long time and thought he was going to die, so Nat asked me to stay on and help look after Mom, who had really bad arthritis."

"Did you like living there? Did you meet anyone?" Mary asked as we headed north off a traffic circle.

"It was difficult. I was in a small fishing town where Lisbonites went in the summer but it was dreary in winter. I ran a medicinal herb shop that Nat set up–it was like a branch of his business, but I owned it. I studied Portuguese and read about herbs. I had few customers and didn't get to know anyone. Everything was so different, especially with children."

"Did they like it?"

"At first. Then when Dad left the hospital, he and Mom moved to a hotel in Lisbon because neither one could cook or shop or do anything, and we moved into their apartment. But the kids in that neighborhood were bullies and after school once a boy sicced a dog on Conrad. And school was hard for Anthony. You wouldn't believe the teachers: they hit him when he didn't get his work done and when I called to say his problem was he didn't know the language, all they said was, 'Well, you know you're free to take him out of our school at anytime.' Eventually, I sent them to their father's in Toronto while I closed down my business."

We stopped talking. My thoughts became consumed with how I was going to cope in Maine. I would have to watch the money I inherited from Mom because I didn't know what to do for work. I still had no skills, not even typing. Having been sick with bronchitis and depression for three months after my divorce, I didn't finish my second year of teaching in Calgary and hence couldn't get my teacher's certificate. Those adorable third-graders sent me all those colorful get-well cards, but I didn't know what to say to the kids after being sick for three months and I couldn't face them. I doubted they'd let me teach in Maine without taking more education courses.

I've been away from the U.S. for twenty-seven years. I know Canadian history and geography, not American, and nothing about the war in Vietnam or the hippie movement of the Sixties. All I do know is that I have to fix up the farmhouse and drive to Toronto for Anthony and Conrad when their school year ends. My kids seem to be doing well, at least their lives are interesting. Anthony's only nine and has been to school in Calgary, Lisbon and Toronto. And Conrad, kindergarten. Now they'll go to school in Kennebunk.

It must be strange for them to have their mother so far away, but at least I'll be able to call from Maine. What'm I going to do in Kennebunk! I'm on my own again.

☙

Upon arriving at Mary's, I stood on the lawn for a couple of minutes to breathe the foggy, salty air, to reaffirm I'd arrived at my childhood haven. The next day Mary and I walked down the beach that I loved so much and hadn't seen since June of 1974, a few months before Nana died. It felt good to be with Mary. We shared the same blue eyes, fair complexion, light hair and small nose characteristic of our extended family's look, and we both had adored our Aunt Llewellyn. These two qualities sufficed to form a warm relationship, even more so because we were in our aunt's old house. On my second day, Mary entertained guests at dinner and every day afterward we did something like shopping, eating at the River Club in Kennebunkport or visiting Saint Ann's by the Sea, the stone church the Bush family attends. She invited me along to her friends' homes for bridge games, luncheons and cocktail parties.

I was surprised that I didn't feel too uncomfortable at these places, but Mary always introduced me to everyone and her friends distracted me with sets of almost identical inquiries about my work and travels. I began to see these questions as their ploy to cope with "different" people.

But after a while I detected a lack of sincerity behind the probing questions because no one ever waited for me to give real answers. After one cocktail party, I felt especially exasperated. I'm just giving a bird's-eye impression, I thought. I'm not saying anything about what my life was really like, that living in Spain wasn't all that rosy, and that after three years, especially when Bobby Kennedy was assassinated and the Spaniards were bad-mouthing Americans more than usual, I hated it, and was desperate to return to the States. But I was too shy to go there alone. I couldn't tell them I married Antonio because he would go with me...well, that wasn't the only reason I married him. I did love him and adored his music, but having someone to go with me to Canada or the United States was more important.

Somehow I sensed Mary's guests would be uncomfortable if I described the bare bones of my life. And besides, I didn't want to reveal too much to them, though I didn't know why. I realize now it would have been inappropriate to talk about such personal matters at parties, especially with people whose lives were so different. Because of my shyness, I'd never been part of a group, and I wasn't cognizant of the factors that distinguish social groups—that people select friends based upon qualities and values they share.

But throughout my stay at Mary's, I always enjoyed her companionship. She was helpful as well as kind; she even arranged for me to meet a woman my age, the daughter of one of her friends. We sat on the beach watching her children. She spoke about her family and especially about her house and entertaining her husband's business friends there. Finding little in common with her and being naturally timid, I said little, churning inside over what I couldn't reveal.

I can't tell her about my mistake-riddled marriage to Antonio, a Venezuelan classical guitarist who spoke little English; that I met him and almost all the people I got to know in Spain at the home of a gay man, about the only place I ever went alone; or about our moving seven times in Calgary, sometimes to dilapidated places; about having no money and having to sell Aunt Llewellyn's diamond brooch to pay for food. Or about Antonio's sleeping with other women and telling me he had a right to because he was Venezuelan. And not for a second do I dare reveal that after we'd agreed to divorce, I stayed with him for three more years, giving birth to a second child, because I was too scared to move out and live by myself.

What would it be like to be part of Mary's group? I'd be forever saying things just to be polite. I remember Dad saying, "Be yourself." I know I'd ruin my chances at it with Mary's crowd. It's one thing not to talk because of shyness; far worse not to speak out of fear my ideas won't fit in. And I

want something more in my social life, something to do with learning, although I've no idea what. I've got to find out.

I lived day by day at Mary's, waiting for someone or something to provide orientation. I took walks around Crescent Surf, enjoying the familiar landscape. After all, this was my reason for being here, that and my heartwarming memories of my grandmother and aunt who'd understood my shyness and tried to help me overcome it.

Out walking around late one foggy morning, I rested on Nana's front porch, thinking about endearing moments with her. Sometimes, after my mother had gone to bed, we would laugh until our stomachs hurt. One of our favorite funny stories revolved around Nana's name–after she married her first cousin, her name changed from Alice Parsons Read to Alice Read Parsons.

On a trip to the Caribbean, a customs official asked for her name, and afterward her maiden one, and when she said it, he eyed her, repeated the question and, being suspicious, told her to sit on an old wooden bench in a dusty office while he conferred with someone. This seems so innocuous today, almost a hundred years later, when custom officials routinely make us remove our shoes to check for explosives.

When I stopped thinking of the good old days the gloomy present loomed. I had no conception of how I wanted my life to be. All I had was a notion that the trees, marshes, and beaches I'd loved so much in my youth could help.

ଔ

To start my new life, I had to brave the few hundred feet to the "farmhouse" that Nat and I inherited from Aunt Llewellyn through our mother.

Colonel Hart acquired Crescent Surf, an area of several hundred acres of land and beaches, soon after the American Revolution. In addition to barns, he built a New England-style Cape Cod house on the only hill, to provide some protection from the sea. Although his house was still called The Farm, no one had done any farming for years and the barns had disappeared completely. The Colonel's descendants sold Crescent Surf to my great-grandfather in 1880 and The Farm sat on one of about thirty lots he created for his heirs.

I'd known the land surrounding The Farm since childhood; the twisted trees in the apple orchard; the hay fields that were now infused with wildflowers; the oak, birch and white pine that seemed larger than life because they grew on a ridge in the distance; the view of the saltwater hay marsh, and beyond, the beautiful ocean. Few people who visit The Farm are untouched by its spiritual aura.

As I trudged up the lane on a raw April morning The Farm's beauty embraced me, calming some of my anxieties about being on my own. I entered the soundless damp house where caretakers had lived until Nana's death.

A massive central chimney with three fireplaces, one for each room downstairs, had served for cooking and heating in colonial times. A set of winding, narrow, high steps led to two bedrooms with slanted ceilings. In the dirt-floor basement, Colonel Hart used a brick root cellar to store food. Later my great-grandfather added a kitchen, laundry room and garage.

For a few weeks I cleaned, returning to Mary's when I got tired, cold or lonely. After I painted the floor a shiny chocolate brown, I needed furniture. When a teenager my mother had often mentioned my having some of the antiques in our house in Prince Edward Island, so I wrote my father now that I was ready to have some. His response taught me one of the most painful lessons I've ever learned about assumptions.

In general I lived by assumptions because I was too inhibited to ask for clarifications. Often these assumptions turned out to be dead wrong; for example, because my parents and other couples seemed happy together, I got married believing it would provide a life of contentment.

And, because of what my mother said when I was a teenager, I assumed I would have some of the antiques that Aunt Llewellyn had bequeathed to us. But for fifteen years I never mentioned it. Now, to my disbelief, my father replied that he and my mother had given away all the furniture years ago to the people who'd bought our house.

Alone on my bed in Mary's big house, I read his letter over and over, failing to understand how my parents neglected to consult with me. I cried as I pictured all the art objects I'd loved and felt connected with, the furniture and ambiance that were still so familiar. They were my childhood, my roots.

Overcome with hurt and anger, I wrote back and insisted that he ask the current owners to give me at least a little of the furniture. He did and they acquiesced. I drove up to P.E.I in a U-haul and collected several pieces they set aside for me. During every minute of the seven-hundred-mile trip, painful thoughts of my family and adolescence haunted me, reminding me of my insignificance.

With the furniture in place, I moved into The Farm feeling a bit more secure, but quite soon became downheart-ed. Having been part of Mary's bustling social life for several weeks, having few social activities depressed me as it had in Portugal. Added to that, the stark contrast between the rustic simplicity of my house and the sophisticated grandeur of Aunt Llewellyn's old place gave me some misgivings about moving to Kennebunk.

I felt confined to my house. Whereas in the 1950s Aunt Llewellyn's and Nana's houses were places where I felt at home, I realized I could never be more than a guest in them now. I felt some envy and anger. I knew I would have to get over it, and soon I did, but it was hard to be so near the homes I loved and not be able to go inside freely.

Nevertheless, that sacred part of us that goads us gently and mitigates our quandaries—something akin to optimism—cheered me up from time to time, allowing me to delight in the knowledge that I now lived on stunning ancestral land, in a charming, historical house with gorgeous antiques. It was my little museum, my treasure. With guidance from Mary, I made curtains and upholstered the sofas and chairs, allowing the measuring, cutting and sewing of beautiful fabrics to energize me. Nevertheless, I couldn't shake the steadfast awareness that I possessed few traits to give shape to a new existence and fewer that would endear me to anyone.

I tried to entertain. I invited Mary and two of her women friends to play bridge. But when they raved about my furni-ture my mouth went dry—I couldn't say anything.

This is so embarrassing. I sure don't want them to know what I had to do to get it and I can't think of anything else to say. It's awful. I'm not at all like these people; they have everything they want and I'm poor and insecure. I don't belong with them. Everyone's waiting for me to say something. I'll bend over, deal the cards and try to pretend it's not necessary to talk.

After they left, I had a couple of drinks. While I was at Mary's I'd regulated my drinking according to what she drank. Now I felt as alone as I'd been in Portugal, and I poured my own, as desperately as I had done there. Indeed my drinking bothered me, but I did it in the afternoons, to relax, before supper, not paying too much attention to it.

Sometimes after supper, not thinking clearly and longing to hear a human voice, I would call someone I'd met at Mary's. I suspected they knew I was drinking because few people asked me to do anything with them or called me back. In a way it was just as well because I often forgot what I'd called about in the first place. However, when I was sober, I didn't know what to say, so I didn't call anyone.

Soon my life was to change, however, with school ending. Time to be a parent again. I was a little nervous. What would it be like to be a mother again? *I've been through so much these past few years. I feel helpless, like I'm at the mercy of others and have no control or knowledge over what I do. I'm like seaweed attached to a sunken ship lying at the bottom of the sea, forever in the waves, going nowhere. My children make me think of the chain of life and that mine's in disrepair, if not broken, first by divorce, then Dad's near death, the loneliness and my mother dying. How can I be a good mother?*

ꝏ

When I first knew I was pregnant, before I told Antonio, doubt plagued me. I couldn't believe I was pregnant! I'd never thought about having children; I didn't know how to take care of myself, how could I look after a child? I knew nothing about babies—I hadn't ever even held one. But when Antonio became overcome with happiness, I felt much relieved. He showered me with more than his usual loving attention and also was emotional toward the unborn child.

When Anthony was six months old, we went to Venezuela and lived with Antonio's huge family for a year (including us, there were seventeen). I observed their loving and caring interactions with one another and I knew why Antonio made a warmer parent than I. Though he never complained about my mothering, on occasion he mentioned he wished I were more outgoing in expressing my love for him.

When we moved to Calgary there was only snow and work with no loving family. Antonio had a part-time job teaching classical guitar, and while I worked at a grueling job in a bank to supplement our income and tended to Anthony, Antonio played at parties and dated other women. Despair thwarted some of my intentions to take better care of myself and my child. So, instead of being more attentive, sometimes I became absorbed with self-pity and anger at myself because shyness kept me inept and unable to leave my philandering husband.

I drove to Toronto, in my square, shock-scanty Fiat, to pick up my sons at their father's apartment. Conrad answered the door. His uncombed blond hair hung down on his face, but I could see his blue eyes sparkling and a wide grin when he hollered, "Hey Anth, Mom's here!" He looked different, dressed in new clothes, and had grown in the last eight months. I was bursting with joy to see him. Then Anthony ran over. His blond-brown hair stood up in curls all over his head and his slender long arms and legs protruded from his Kmart clothes. I saw at once how happy they were to see me. I hugged them both in one embrace, one in each arm. This was my family, my flesh and blood, my love and all that really mattered to me in the whole world!

Antonio asked me all about my father and mother, Portugal and Kennebunk. Anthony, nine, and Conrad, six, chimed in with what they knew. I asked about their schools and friends. It was possible they had some misgivings about leaving their father, but they didn't let on.

When it came time to start for Maine, Antonio told his children he loved them, would miss them and would visit in August. Fortunately for me, although he cared for his children dearly, there was no doubt in his mind that they belonged with their mother–in Venezuela mothers looked after the children.

In spite of having almost no money and living in yet another apartment with nothing but a simple kitchen table set, egg crates for storage and the floor to sleep on, Antonio still exudes an air of everything I crave: energy, joy, and accomplishment. I don't think it's possible for me to be like that. Could I? Compared with him, I've got no personality and nothing exciting happening in my life.

After hearing many times "Are we almost there yet?" I watched for Conrad and Anthony's facial expressions when they first saw their new home. Their eyes lit up. Running inside, glancing left and right, they dashed around before going upstairs, where they decided who was to get which bedroom. They went out, turning around, gawking, yelling, "Wow, cool! Can we have bikes?" I was glad they were happy and relieved to have them with me, at last.

☙

On July Fourth the relatives who had also inherited property in Crescent Surf came to vacation and the socializing began. I'd always visited Nana and Aunt Llewellyn in June or September, the off-season, when only a few cousins visited, so I didn't know most of them. I'd never even seen them at a party.

The first gathering I attended was a lively one. I inched my way into a little circle of cousins reminiscing with gusto about unknown-to-me people and events. They greeted me pleasantly, but shortly returned their focus to each other. I learned they'd known one another since childhood and that many got together where they lived year-round.

Remaining at the party, but not being a part of it, I studied people's appearances. Most of them looked like guests I'd seen at Mary's: clean-shaven men with trim haircuts, dressed in colorful pants and jackets with neckties covered with little images such as golf balls representing their hobbies. The women looked well groomed and wore stylish dresses and eye-catching necklaces, earrings and bracelets. I did nothing special with my hair or makeup and my clothing tended to be of a simpler sort with few accessories.

I saw most of the same relatives at about half a dozen parties. At first I didn't feel of lesser worth in spite of their yachts, social networks and links to places such as Harvard and Yale. I believed we were sort of on an equal footing because of our common ancestry. But, reluctantly and with great disappointment, I saw no one seemed genuinely interested in me and being related didn't count for much. I had no idea of how to deal with this underlying feeling of exclusion, and I drank more than I should at the gatherings.

I can see today just how different I was. In addition to dressing with no notion of style except for my own—I still dress that way, but my style is better developed—I spoke rapidly, often blurting things out, with a Canadian accent. But what probably turned my cousins off more than anything was the same problem that ruined my conversations with everyone: inhibitions and lack of conversational skills. I had little idea what to talk about and no social savvy with which to speak when I did think of something. In addition I lacked language skills. I'd spoken in Spanish with Antonio for six years and my English, having never been very good, suffered. When listening, I understood few expressions, but didn't like to ask for clarifications.

But on Labor Day the relatives departed as quickly as they'd appeared and then I saw a different Maine, the Maine of the other ten months, without summer people dominating everything. With few relatives around, it became almost too quiet at Crescent Surf, although I was glad I didn't have to compare myself with anyone. While my children attended public schools with excellent reputations, the school district called me to substitute two or three times a week.

A pervasive loneliness slowly set in when I was home alone. Eventually I got up the courage to go to the duplicate bridge club which I enjoyed although most people were older. One elderly bridge partner invited me to go to the Unitarian church—it had been my father's religion—and I jumped at the chance to see if there Anthony, Conrad and I might get to have friends.

Conrad helped break the ice the first Sunday morning. While sitting in a pew, he kept a hunter's-orange hat pulled over his forehead, almost covering his eyes, attracting everyone's attention. Following the service during coffee hour, with his hat pulled up and his face now beaming, many people spoke with him. Anthony found someone his age to talk with. They were invited to and agreed to attend Sunday School.

I craved knowledge and intellectual rapport and joined a discussion group. But the half-dozen people there, mostly men, seemed to be experts at thinking through their thoughts and making rapid responses. Since I wasn't quick enough to get a word in, after a few of sessions I gave up.

Dread of going to church or anyplace where I was expected to talk with others bothered me at least twenty-four hours in advance. I pushed myself to go, though, because I thought over time the fear would diminish and I so wanted to see others, to be with people!

One Sunday at coffee, I listened to an informal discussion about going to war in Vietnam. Someone remarked that you shouldn't have to defend your country if you don't believe in the war's cause. To my horror, I was unable to formulate ideas about the war and was embarrassed and shocked by my limited understanding of important concepts such as duty and courage.

What was the matter with me? Why couldn't I grasp the meanings of these words? Hadn't I been intelligent in school? In addition to being shy, I knew now for certain I had no philosophy and felt more inferior because of it.

ଓ

At church, someone introduced me to Roland Rose. Six feet tall and lanky, at first he appeared bookish; he had straight hair, glasses, a sizable nose and serious expression. When he turned to say hello, his hair fell onto his face and his expression exploded into wholeheartedness. I thought, *I wish I were married to him!*

Then, by chance, in mid-September I saw him again at a Psy Symposium, a meeting of about twenty, mostly Unitarians, who gathered monthly at different people's homes to hear a guest share experiences with extra-terrestrial happenings, followed by a discussion.

With people everywhere, during the potluck supper that preceded the meeting, I found myself sitting on the floor beside Roland. Soon we began talking and he said, "I live in Kennebunk, but I work up and down the East Coast."

"What do you do?" I asked after I took a sip of red wine.

"Many things, actually–several types of consulting jobs in different places; once, in Key West, Florida, I was in charge of developing a plan to train Navy personnel on race relationships. In New Hampshire I gave workshops for caregivers of patients suffering from drug addiction."

He filled our wine glasses while we ate spaghetti, salad and broccoli. He looked contented, sitting cross-legged in his blue jeans with a light-colored shirt tucked in at the waist.

Goodness, what sort of person is this? I've never talked with anyone as interesting as this. He's so casual too; bet he's not hard to get to know.

I prodded him along. “How do you know how to do all those different types of things?” Twirling the stem of his glass slowly, he responded, “I got a Master’s in Public Administration at New York University, which helped me learn theories of organization. That’s what it’s really all about.”

When I was silent, he went on, “I studied with financial assistance from the Army and when the Korean War broke out the Army Reserve Unit called me. During some rapid-fire coursework, I got promoted to Sergeant Major and set up to be in charge of the intelligence and propaganda unit slated for Korea. Then in typical military fashion, the orders changed and they shipped us to Germany. Following the war, I did what I really wanted to do, I went to Spain to paint!”

Aha! at last I saw we had something in common, and I piped up, “Oh, I went to Spain, too, after University!” and I talked about living in Madrid for four years and visiting several Spanish cities.

After supper we sat in a circle giving me a chance to observe the others. The women tended to have on loose-fitting, colorful layered garments, but one or two just wore jeans and a simple blouse as I did. The men had on jeans or shorts, sandals, and several people smoked. Neither Roland nor I said anything during the animated discussion that followed the guest’s talk.

When I said goodnight to him, I didn't expect to see much of him in the future because, to my dismay, he’d mentioned he had a family.

But the universe had designed other plans for me. When I got into my Fiat, the key wouldn't fit the ignition and, upon inspection back inside the house, it appeared decidedly twisted.

"What else could it be but a supernatural force!" exclaimed a few lingering people, including Roland.

A firm believer in serendipity, Roland took this as a signal for him to drive me home and for us to get to know each other better. He told me about not sleeping with his wife for over a year and that he only stayed with her for the kids, but now the three oldest were pretty independent, with boyfriends or husbands. The next day Roland put a typed letter in my mailbox, saying he hoped I didn't mind that he was married, because he wanted to see me. He phoned later to see if he could visit.

Sometimes he brought coffee, and he introduced me to bagels with cream cheese. He didn't ask a lot of questions or make conversational demands and I felt comfortable. We usually stayed around my place, sometimes crisscrossing over footpaths in the woods savoring autumn and at times driving over to Kennebunkport, empty now of tourists, to have an ice-cream cone and see the fishing boats. It was easy to get to know him in such tranquil settings.

Strolling on our beach one day, listening to the gentle lap of small waves fill the silence, suddenly Roland interrupted the cadence. "You'll have to get something for the winter, you know, to heat your house. It gets really cold. We could go to Sanford, if you like, and look at woodstoves."

Wow, I can't believe it—I have someone to help me! He's got experience and knows what to do. Just what I need.

Shortly after we installed the woodstove, he suggested we paint my house. For days we scraped the two hundred-year-old clapboards and later applied a slightly deeper tone of yellow than it had been and painted the window frames in barn red. Most important, we enjoyed each other's company, smiling while reaping rewards from making something old look new.

Roland visited every day and I was falling in love. I counted the moments until I would see him, of when he would hold me next, of wondering what he would say about this, about that. My general attitude morphed from being lonely and uncertain about what to do, to feeling loved and having plenty of things to look forward to.

At the end of the day, when I relaxed indoors and the children played outside, when the brilliant fiery glow from the sun penetrated the white pines into the den, I wanted Roland near. He wanted to be with me, too. He filed for divorce, and in November, in time for Thanksgiving, came to live with us.

ꙮ

The day after St. Valentine's, a day after Roland gave me a beautiful pink suit, I sat close to him, holding his hand, watching the news. During a break, I said, "I wish I knew more people." "Yeah," he said. "Sometimes it's hard... Look at that, China's invading Vietnam again."

I was taken aback that he wasn't interested in talking about feelings, which meant I couldn't talk about mine with him. I might have tried to say something more and perhaps ameliorated some of my inner turmoil, but I didn't.

That night I couldn't fall asleep. ***I never make goals for myself like Roland does. I'm afraid to; I focus on what could go wrong. When I try to do things, I feel too shy to do what I want, and that causes me to abandon ideas.*** I established a pattern of directing my attention to Roland and his needs when he was present. I feared he might not like me if I didn't and leave me. It became like a necessity—as if his needs were more essential than anyone else's.

But that meant when Roland was present my children had to wait until I was alone for me to spend quality time with them. One day while I was sitting with him, Conrad came in with a question. "Mom, for my birthday can I get a model airplane? Can I come with you to get it?" "I don't know. Let me think about it." I didn't want to focus on Conrad's needs with Roland there. My children never complained about not receiving more attention from me and I wonder why not. But then, as a child I generally accepted my parents' behavior, even when I didn't like it.

Doing breakfast dishes Sunday, I saw Roland shovel snow to help Anthony reach his skis. They seemed to get along—maybe we do make a good family, I thought. And Anthony has a good friend from school coming over to ski with him. Blindsided by the loneliness I remembered during my childhood, I focused on one driving goal for Anthony and Conrad: to see they had friends.

All winter everything outdoors was either white or brown. By spring we were ecstatic to see grass sprouting and specks on branches swell into buds. By June the ocean turned many shades of blue, my favorite being dark sapphire dappled with glittering sunshine.

Anthony, Conrad and I—Roland tended to stay indoors writing proposals for consulting work that never came through—developed exciting plans to use of some of our land. We purchased two pink baby pigs along with a curly-haired, small brown lamb and planted a huge vegetable garden. Then I bought six fuzzy Gray Lag goslings because I'd loved our geese in Prince Edward Island and also because Antonio and I had named Conrad after Dr. Konrad Lorenz, Swiss author of books about the complex social lives of geese.

Our St. Bernard, Brutus, astonished us by demonstrating Lorenz's theory of bird imprinting with the goslings. He became the birds' "parent," and they slept cuddled up in his long, bushy tail. If he happened to be nurturing the goslings when we went outdoors, instead of bounding over to us in recognition, he simply raised his head as high as he could, twisting his neck around to see us. All day long the goslings trailed after him, for three months, and then either the dog or the geese decided to end the strange relationship.

Anthony, now ten, loved to spend time in nature. Sometimes he collected a pocketful of baby snakes, and they would stay on his palm while he stroked them and talked to them. He hunted red squirrels and small birds using a .22-caliber air rifle. He made a photographic story of shooting a red squirrel: getting the gun, walking to the woods, aiming, holding his trophy and nailing the little animal's pelt out to dry on a board. Indoors he spent hours doing Lego and making model cars and airplanes.

Conrad, now seven, liked being with people more than nature and he astonished me with his social insight. For example, once he bought two small ratty-looking teddy bears at the Unitarian Universalist Church yard sale, and his facial expression indicated that by this purchase he was now part of U.U. tradition.

His teacher at school told me he was doing well in spite of attending special classes to overcome dyslexia. "Often when kids leave their home room for extra help, their classmates taunt them when they return, but it doesn't happen with Conrad. He's very popular."

One day I picked him up early for a doctor's appointment and I saw why she said that. As we walked down the long corridor, other kids who happened to be present stood still, as if mesmerized, watching Conrad pass by. Most greeted him: "Bye, Conrad."

What does he do to get this mysterious connectedness with his classmates? They adore him. I was so very different, no one ever spoke to me in school—I wouldn't have known how to handle it if they had. People still don't talk to me. How did I get to have a son like this? This is as close as I've ever been to popularity—trailing down a hallway behind Conrad.

☙

A year passed and, when not helping me on household improvements, Roland spent most of his time thinking about how to make money. He had little and I was using my inheritance for our household costs.

Because none of his local consulting proposals came through, he applied for a high-paying position in Los Angeles. He didn't say what would happen to us if he got it, whether the children and I would join him or what. I suspected maybe not, but I didn't dare ask, afraid to know. He flew out for an interview and wasn't accepted, but I was left with doubt and a feeling of powerlessness.

One morning he came into the den where I was making a list of things to do and Brutus was napping at my feet. "This is kind of interesting: here's an ad for the H and R Block Income Tax Franchise in Kennebunk. Look," he said, creasing the newspaper, "H and R Block provides instruction and we can take the classes and work at this business together. You've got to put up the money because I don't have any, but I'll put in experience as my share since I want to be an equal partner."

Thinking intently, I replied, "I guess so, as long as we only have one bank account for the earnings and I get to spend all I need for household expenses."

If Block teaches us how to do it, how could his business experience be that important? What an odd, illogical way he thinks. But what do I care as long as I get to spend the income. I need him and love the idea of working with him, so I'll go along with it. Besides, I don't want to do anything to cause him to move away.

I'd substituted at four schools during the winter and found it difficult. Memories of my last experience at a junior high school still disturbed me. I'd never related well to teenagers, not even while I was one. I'd formed no close bonds with any and now as a teacher I eyed them suspiciously; they seemed unruly, unreliable and sometimes even offensive.

One afternoon two kids saw my anxiety and in direct disobedience snickered and laughed with each other. I saw one boy deliberately drop his pencil on the floor so he could lean over to pick it up near his classmate and whisper with him; they looked at me and pretended to choke down laughter. After the bell rang I broke down, weeping just a little, but not before all of the kids had left. I felt embarrassed—defeated—and didn't go back to that school.

And so the H and R Block business idea appealed to me and we bought the franchise. I'd rarely seen an income tax form and had never filled one out, but Roland helped me understand Block's instructions in ways I could manage, and later he set up our office procedure. So, contrary to my expectations, I actually did rely on his help many times in running the business. And we did well; our franchise grew fivefold during the ten years we owned it.

I loved numbers and working with them focused my attention, allowing me to forget my social anxieties, but I developed no friendships at work. Because of my timidity, I couldn't suggest to clients I found interesting that we do something together besides income taxes. Only one woman, Diane, whom I met at work, became a friend, and that was only after I left H and R Block.

Diane struck me as an exceptionally warm person and she also impressed me with her approach to her taxes. She wouldn't take a back seat to money and, instead of filing with the tax status "married" as almost all couples do, she insisted on filing "married-filing separately" even though it cost her several hundred dollars extra in taxes. I did my best to persuade her not to file that way.

"No, Helen," she insisted each year, "this is an official record of the money I make. I want it because it shows I'm making money on my own, that I support myself."

I was mystified by the feeling of inner strength emanating from her. While she spoke, I shuffled papers on my desk pretending to look at numbers, but I wasn't. *She knows what's important to her, what she wants and insists on doing it; it's not important that she doesn't understand accounting. How I wish I knew how to be like that. I don't have a clue about what's important to me.*

ଓ

Two years into the income tax business, it had become my habit to rush home from work, sometimes carrying groceries, exhausted from the hours and precision my work demanded. Anthony, now twelve, would be putting together a model or working with Lego; Conrad, nine, might be talking on the phone. I went straight to doing housework, without giving them much more than a rapid greeting. They weren't in a rush for supper because they'd already had snacks.

Fed up with this pace, one beautiful afternoon, I rescheduled a couple of appointments and went home early. I climbed our four wooden steps bordered by skeletons of baby's breath bushes covered here and there with light snow, and once inside the sunny kitchen I saw Anthony leave for the living room. Delighted to be home early, I rushed straight to him to say hello. But instead of seeing pleasure on his face, I saw red lines in his eyes and smelled gin on his breath. He looked downward, put his glass behind him and neither of us spoke. Alarm bells rang out, but too timid and uncertain of what to say, I hurried to my bedroom.

My child drinking! My beloved first child drinks! He comes home from school and drinks! I must have set a bad example with my own drinking. What can I do? I have to get something for him to do ... so he won't feel the need to drink. Oh, how terrible. What would help—what would he like. Think, Helen, think. Maybe play the piano—his father and grandmother were musicians, and as a child I'd always wanted to play.

In a couple of days I asked him if he'd like to learn to play the piano and he said yes. So I bought a small used one and found a teacher to give him lessons. He seemed good at playing, and practiced diligently.

I didn't learn why Anthony drank because I was too scared to broach the topic. I forgot about the gin. I focused my attention on seeing him play. I wanted my children to have achievements in life, to develop talents, to experience what I'd missed. Providing the piano lessons was my first accomplishment to that end.

It's clear I didn't see Anthony for whom he was because I was too self-absorbed. In spite of the gin, I thought he was well liked in school and had no problems. Years later he told me he hadn't fit in well with his classmates because he was thin and had pimples. He also told me, "I wished I'd had better clothes."

The fall I bought the piano, 1980, our home became splendid. With volunteer assistance from a community group that promoted alternative power, we built a passive solar greenhouse. With help from the local power conservation department, we had insulation blown into the walls and new storm windows installed. We bought a newly invented type of woodstove, a slow-burning one that would give off heat for twelve hours without adding logs. I kept the antique furniture polished and Anthony played his piano.

Then after lunch on February 24, 1981, while Roland and I worked and Anthony and Conrad studied, a stranger knocked on the office door with a message that forever changed every single thing in my life.

"Sorry to have to tell you this; we tried calling you, but your phone's not working. Your house is on fire."

7

The Push

It takes ten minutes to drive home from Kennebunk on the narrow, tree-arched road I'd loved since childhood. It was one of those times when I wanted to separate from my mind, not to think, but that process wouldn't stop. A fire truck on the Crescent Surf Beach Road confirmed, "Fire, destruction!" I barely managed to get my lightweight Pinto up the lane because water-bearing trucks had ground it into a mixture of snow, sand and water.

Around the curve at the top, I saw an enormous cloud where my house should be. The fuzzy air wasn't just from freezing rain, but also from truckloads of water striking the flames. There was barely a break between the ground and the gray-white floating mass, but in that tiny seam I saw absolutely nothing. My home was gone.

Just a few firemen were present, dousing embers. Volunteer fire departments from five towns had fought valiantly, but with the nearest fire hydrant over a mile away and with narrow, slippery dirt roads, it was an impossible mission.

Remaining back and out of the way, I stood in a foot of snow under drenching sleet, transfixed. Brutus performed what the Saint Bernard is bred for: to keep the injured upright and moving so they don't collapse and freeze in mountainous regions. He did this by circling me crazily, again and again, brushing my legs, looking up at me, and he didn't stop until I patted his head and said, "Hi, Brutus. Good dog, good dog," thereby letting him know I was all right.

If only Brutus could talk, he would have told me about big trucks barreling up the hill, sliding around in his yard and about men dressed in yellow and black running everywhere around his home. Fortunately, as usual, the dog had spent the day outside while we were at work, but the cats normally stayed inside to sleep on our beds. The firemen told me that they probably died right away from smoke inhalation.

After a couple of hours, around four in the afternoon, Anthony and Conrad appeared and ran over to me, their eyes smudged with dark streaks from wiping tears. Unbeknownst to me, a first cousin, Debbie, picked them up from school to warn them of the fire, so the sight would be less shocking to them.

I hardly knew Debbie; she was four years older than I, and we rarely did anything together as a twosome. I'd seen her at family parties, but we'd spoken little. Quite unlike me, she appeared to be influenced by tradition, but I deeply appreciated her forethought and help in picking up my children from school. I'd been too distraught to even think about doing that.

Conrad said, "What a mess! I'm glad my bike's being fixed." Anthony was more aware of the totality of our loss; he looked grim, said nothing. I didn't know what to say, either; I could think of nothing to console them. I kept my head down as if to say this phase of our lives is over and I don't know what to do now. I was unable to be comforting and felt inadequate.

Debbie broke the silence and offered immediate relief. "I'm so sorry. Spend the night with us and then you can stay in the Sandpiper until June." Owned by her two sisters, their house was right on the ocean, a little to the east of Debbie's home.

Shortly, she drove away taking Anthony and Conrad with her. I stayed, wishing it wasn't happening, wanting to be a part of my home for as long as I could, for as long as a tiny bit of it was left. I felt I'd never recover from this; I'd lost everything from the past, picture albums and letters with my mother and grandmother's handwriting. I'd never see their handwriting again! Or Aunt Llewellyn's! I'd lost everything that belonged to the people I loved.

Finally, around five, Roland arrived in his Pinto station wagon: he'd stayed at the office to attend to clients. By now colder air had caused much of the mist to lift and he saw nothing more than a few charred beams lying crisscrossed, semi-covered in ash. He dashed up to me saying, "Oh, Helen. No, no!" I cried inside his arms.

In a few minutes, just before dark, I remembered another precious heirloom. The firemen had told me to stay away from the steaming ashes, but I couldn't resist looking for it. I went to the granite block where the front door had stood, carefully inched my way over a couple of feet of simmering coals to where the closet had been, stooped over and saw the tiniest spec of bright turquoise, Nana's engagement pin. Although it was mostly destroyed, this near impossible discovery buoyed me up. I knew Lady Luck hadn't abandoned me altogether.

Normally we walked everywhere at Crescent Surf; it seemed odd to go to Debbie's in two cars. In ways my children and Roland seemed like strangers: this calamity required every ounce of my concentration, leaving little attention for them. I hugged Anthony and Conrad; I cried but had few words. That evening they sat together watching television, and I didn't ask what they were thinking. Soon the phone started ringing and some cousins and an acquaintance from church expressed sympathy. I called Nat; it was his house, too. He said little but asked that I keep him informed. I think I asked him to tell our father.

Around nine I gave Anthony and Conrad another hug and kissed them goodnight. Numb from emotional exhaustion as well as scotch, once in bed I huddled beside Roland and fell asleep, knowing that in the morning the kids would go to school, Roland would go to the office, and I would buy supplies—one of everything, starting from scratch.

☙

On the Sunday following the fire, the Unitarian Universalist Church took up a special collection for us, and, when I was leaving, a woman offered to give me counsel.

Like a robot, I kept walking, without even looking at her for more than a second. The idea of discussing my problems with her caused me to panic. I didn't know how to respond to her offer and that made me lose control over my senses. This reaction had occurred a few times in the past, such as when Nat prevented the doctor from removing his tonsils. I was bothered by it, but I thought I couldn't do anything about it.

Weeks later, walking down my lane with a cousin who was a pastor, I received another offer to help. I stared at the oak branches overhead, unable to say anything. A voice inside snatched my attention: *I haven't mourned my mother. I haven't dealt with my feelings about my painful upbringing, and now I'm so emotionally raw it's like my outer skin has peeled off. My home, my belongings, my identity are gone. What on earth do I say without totally breaking down and revealing how miserable I am?*

ᘓ

As most severely shy people know, one of the worst consequences of shyness is being unable to talk about yourself. If I'd learned how to be close to people, to make friends, my childhood pain might have lessened years earlier. Not knowing how to make friends stunted my social and emotional growth more than anything else. Because I had no one to share my experiences with, I didn't learn how to express myself, which in turn decimated my self-confidence.

Today, professionals know the necessity for and how to help shy children learn to play and talk with peers. As a child I was mortified about my shyness and couldn't mention it; as an adult, I was so embarrassed by it that I couldn't ask for or accept help.

A recently completed study by Tara Parker-Pope (reported in the *New York Times*, April 9, 2009) says that so much has been said about lovers and marriage, but very little about friendships. This follows:

> Last year, researchers studied thirty-four students, taking them to the base of a steep hill and fitting them with a weighted backpack.

> They were then asked to estimate the steepness of the hill. Some participants stood next to friends during the exercise, while others were alone.
>
> The students who stood with friends gave lower estimates of the steepness of the hill. And the longer the friends had known each other, the less steep the hill appeared.

☙

The fire occurred during the height of the tax season and, to get my mind off it, I focused on work. Mostly I was in a daze, from working with numbers in the daytime and from drinking alcohol in the evenings. Anthony and Conrad went to school, built Lego models and watched television. We didn't commiserate much. With little heart, I helped with their food, transportation and some shopping.

I seemed to be with Roland continuously. I watched him busy himself at home, at work and couldn't figure him out: nothing fazed him, not even the fire. I never saw him stare off into space as I did when I felt lost or lonely. He was older and more experienced, but the fact that he didn't seem to need to share feelings or to have friends perplexed me.

From time to time, it occurred to me that maybe we could discuss ways to have a better social life, but I didn't know how to phrase it. Instead, sitting with Roland on the couch in front of the fireplace at the Sandpiper, our temporary home, all I did was to implore once again, "But, Roland, we don't have any friends! I want friends!"

"Helen, I can't help you there; I don't know how to make friends myself. I'm poor at relationships, and I don't express emotions well. But," he said, turning to look at me, "I've been thinking about what we could do to rebuild. I suggest we put out a bid in various newspapers to ask for ideas from architects, for a house on the same location as the old one. We only have to pay the architect whose plan we select."

"Okay, yes, sounds like a good idea." ***Damn, what a clever way to skirt my problem. I wish he'd pay more attention to my needs...he just won't.***

I'd never thought about building a house and had no idea what design I wanted. In my distraught state, I had little inclination to think about it, so I was relieved when Roland took the initiative. I had no option but to ignore that he wouldn't address my personal needs.

I worried about money. We'd been way underinsured and only received a few thousand dollars for landscaping, a little more for furniture, and not much for the house itself. Roland suggested I take out a mortgage with Nat, because he was part owner. Nat agreed.

☙

Just before we left the Sandpiper in June, a fellow Unitarian offered us the use of an old trailer, and because it was so small, Anthony and Conrad flew to Calgary to stay with Antonio for the summer. We sited it on the hill, within thirty feet of the charred rafters and piles of ashes.

At first I didn't go near the ruins. Then one day I stepped down the short aluminum camper ladder, walked straight to the debris and, on my knees, starred into it. I saw myself in the ashes and thought of the expression, "There, but by the grace of God, go I." But even alive, I felt helpless.

I craved companionship, but that summer not one relative visited me to offer consolation. I even heard that some of the cousins who lived elsewhere in winter insinuated that trailers were illegal at Crescent Surf. I didn't mention it to Roland because I knew he would only complain about the relatives and not sympathize with me, which was what I wanted.

I tried to block out thoughts about my cousins. I cried a lot: nothing in my life seemed to make sense. Apart from nature and the serenity it gave me, Roland, in his cool cerebral way, was my sole caregiver.

I know now that neither Roland nor anyone else knew how much I suffered from shyness and its ramifications. My relatively good looks, work experience, knowledge of three languages and my above-average intelligence may have covered up my inhibitions. It was even possible I gave off an air of self-containment and, with their busy lives, my cousins decided to leave me alone.

Because I wasn't in the habit of exploring matters, I didn't learn until fall that our insurance company would pay for our lodging during reconstruction. In time for Thanksgiving 1981, we moved uptown to the Kennebunk Inn where the four of us enjoyed its casual, historic atmosphere and proximity to schools and work.

The construction was coming along and we visited several times a week to see what was needed. During one of those visits in late spring, while my children were at school, I experienced my first–at least the first of which I was cognizant–spurt of personal growth, the result of a little mishap. In order to save money on carpenters, Roland and I stained about half a dozen pine doors on the front lawn. I noticed an ache in my back that slowly worsened. I ignored it, and by late afternoon, I lay sprawled on the ground, unable to move.

My doctor said he could do nothing, and sent me to see a chiropractor. A chiropractor? What exactly was that? It felt daring. Upon examination, the chiropractor noticed a structural deformity in my spine, and recommended exercising, including balancing a book on my head when I walked. I'd always slouched, the result of being tall, skinny and shy.

Now I had to stand straight, making me feel as if I were showing off. I worked at it, and in a few weeks I stood a little taller. For the first time I became aware that some people pursued specific activities in order to grow as a person. I was too put off, though, and afraid, by the thought of examining my weak areas, and I didn't seek more growth opportunities.

☙

Finally our house was ready, and in December 1982, after living out of boxes in several locations for twenty months, we moved in. Nothing about our new home replicated the old one, except for the foundation. A cathedral ceiling extended over three living areas defined only by furniture: a den, a dining room, and a living room with a fireplace. Because of the generous size allocated to that big room, the three bedrooms were smallish. Wide decks with seating and planters lined the east and west of the house. We stained the outside pine clapboards a light, dull blue and named our home The Great Blue Heron, after some of the birds that flew overhead and fished in the marsh. To my surprise and delight, the old house went out of my mind and I felt better about its loss.

Roland was my locomotive; he was full of direction and energy, and I loved that about him. Every day while I drank my first cup of coffee, he came up with many ideas–about work, a future trip or just errands. I went along with his suggestions, always by his side, in bed, at the table, in the car and at the office. It seemed natural and good for me. I had few, if any plans of my own and I embraced his. Yet, I still suffered from loneliness and it upset me that my children stayed by themselves after school until six or seven, just like they had in Portugal when I worked. I didn't know what to do about it.

Not wanting to risk upsetting Roland, rather than ask for changes, I rationalized that the success of our business was paramount for everyone. I didn't know what I would do if Roland were to leave and, I believed my children were doing fine with not too much attention from me. When I did feel brave enough to leave Roland's side for a few hours, I took Anthony and Conrad to the movies, to stores to buy equipment for fishing, cycling and hunting and, a couple of times drove them to the White Mountains, during all of which I felt like a better parent.

ᘓ

One year after moving into our new home, in 1983, I realized I couldn't cover my share of the mortgage and property taxes. I'd worried when we were building about the money it was costing, but I went along with Roland's suggestions believing that he knew best and I didn't want to be critical for fear he might get mad. I failed to speak up in a timely fashion and I let us build a house we couldn't afford. ***Damn, I never speak when I should.***

We resorted to what many Mainers do who live near the ocean: rent the house for top dollar during the summer. I became exhausted from putting personal belongings away and cleaning everything before Roland and I moved into our office in Kennebunk and Anthony and Conrad visited again with their father. All summer I missed my children and my new home, feeling economically poor for having to live this way.

During a makeshift supper in the office, Roland suggested I sell a few acres of land.

No one has ever sold land at Crescent Surf and I treasure every square inch of it. The idea repulses me! But wait. It makes no sense to me either if I have to be someplace else because I can't afford to live here.

Land is so strange. No one can really own it–I only have it for now. And if I didn't own it, it would still be here. But nearby construction would ruin the tranquility–spoil the view too. Roland is not attached to the property like I am. I really hate to sell any of it–it connects me to this area, the only connection I've got anywhere to anything. But I need money.

Voicing none of my concerns, I went along with Roland's suggestions and Nat agreed. By now I'd worked under Roland's direction for four years, first on house projects–the old one and then the new one and at work. It seemed natural that he set the course for how we could sell land.

We made plans to form a subdivision near Route 9, on the part of our property that was as far away as possible from anybody's home, so it wouldn't upset anyone's serenity, including our own, or so we thought. But when it came time to discuss selling this land with my relatives, my poor conversational abilities–lack of verbal clarity and failure to speak up forcefully–caused no end to misunderstandings. Gossip took over. The worst rumor, the one that pitted everyone against me, was that we were selling rights to the beach.

I hurt. I ached from losing my old house, from the need to sell some of my beloved land and now from neighborhood disdain. I needed love and caring from my relatives: they were, after all, living reminders of Nana and Aunt Llewellyn. But they didn't give it and I recoiled; hatred seethed in my veins. I sat alone in my beautiful house.

Roland sat down to talk with me in the kitchen while I made lunch. "Why don't we move?" he said, helping me cut the string beans, "We don't have to stay here where people cause you so much pain. Sell this and buy where you'll be comfortable."

"No, I don't want to!"

I couldn't say anything more. Roland didn't understand. In hindsight, I see that I was so shy and tight-lipped that I hadn't even told him I'd come to Kennebunk to be near the memories of Nana and Aunt Llewellyn, the two people who had demonstrated an endearing love for me and who understood my lonely, perennial battle with social awkwardness. I wanted to remain near where they'd lived for whatever inspiration they might still provide me and for the calming effect of the beauty of the land. Also, if I had roots anywhere, they were here at Crescent Surf, and I didn't want to lose that.

With no one who could give me emotional comfort, I set off to the ocean to see if I could make some sense of it. The miniature waves rolled at my feet. I rounded the end of the beach where Little River carves its passage to the ocean and

I nestled into a sandy embankment ten feet above the current. My eyes roamed the vast green marsh upriver, framed by beautiful trees until they became specs. Downriver dozens of hungry terns, plovers and seagulls circled above the ocean on the lookout for food. Land purchased by my great-grandfather surrounded me.

Generations of relatives have enjoyed this beach as I am today. Nana would have had a fit if she was here–she wouldn't let me be in the position I'm in now. People would have listened to her. The trouble now is that no one person is in control–everyone does what they want to satisfy their own interests–no one cares about everyone, as Nana did. The scariest thing is that each person thinks so differently; it's hard to imagine what their interests might be in the future. It's hard to see people ever pulling together.

So, I opted to sell some land to be able to afford to stay at Crescent Surf. Soon the three cousins forbid Nat and me from accessing our beach without their permission, and one told me I didn't deserve access to it, a comment that sufficed to shock me into finally getting help.

Sometimes I wonder whether I would ever have made it into counseling without my home burning down, causing me to need money, which prompted my cousin's caustic remark, which in turn pushed me to a psychologist. I doubt it. I don't believe that things "happen for a purpose," but I do believe that when a crisis occurs, it gives us an opportunity for growth.

8

Counsel and Epiphany

A week after I decided to seek help, in July of 1984, I met with Kathleen Cussick, a Stanford PhD in psychology, my age and a newcomer to Kennebunk. Incredibly, she lived and worked in the basement apartment of the Storer Mansion, the house where my great-grandfather was born.

As I entered the room, all I could think about was my good fortune in meeting my counselor within the very walls where my great-grandfather lived. I felt him in the air trying to comfort me!

Kathleen sat me down on a comfortable sofa, positioned herself across from me on an easy chair, and said, "How do you think I can help you, Helen?"

Bursting into tears, I said, "I don't get along with my relatives." Crying during the entire session, I described the chaos of the previous few years. I knew the uncontrollable sobbing came mainly from childhood wounds, not the recent past, but I was too shy to say so. I can see now how this failure may have really slowed my growth, but for me it required a monumental effort just to divulge recent problems.

Kathleen radiated warmth and understanding. Below her light auburn fluffed hair and large freckled forehead, her light-brown eyes beamed at me. Her well-enunciated diction trickled like a sonorous stream, but when she explained certain ideas, her voice touched every note of a full octave. She held a large fountain pen in her white hand and looked at me expectantly.

She seemed brilliant, as if she were an extension of the stacks of books on her tables, chairs and floor. What I liked most about my first session was that I myself would participate in the healing process. "It's a two-step process, Helen. First we've got to gut the old harmful habits and then bring in healthy ones to take their place."

Driving home, I thought about the session. *I feel like a different person. Stronger. Braver. All those years thinking it would be dreadfully embarrassing to get help, but sitting with Kathleen in her office wasn't so hard at all. It seemed more like a natural thing to do. I'm so relieved. I've done it—at last I've done it...and in my great grandfather's home! It seems as though it was meant to be.*

At the house, Roland was waiting, standing by the fireplace looking serious. He questioned what Kathleen and I discussed. He'd told me before how his first wife had changed after she learned about women's liberation. I didn't understand much, if anything, about that, but I hoped Kathleen wasn't propelling me in that direction. I told him what we talked about, and he seemed all right with it.

In my third session, Kathleen asked me to describe my relationships. My eyes jerked around, my mouth opened and shut, but I couldn't say anything.

Then she explained the importance of relationships and suggested I work on developing some. It was strange to hear someone describe me, analyze me, and, especially, try to help me. I sank deeper into the soft sofa, dared relax a little and allowed myself to think about what she'd just asked me.

I looked at my world and relationships. I felt like a scared baby bird barely daring to peep out of the nest. I saw faces of people with whom I'd communicated over a period of years, but try as I might I couldn't recall many mutual bonds or supportive feelings with anyone. I'd blanked out of my mind how very alone I felt because it was so awfully painful to acknowledge it.

In hindsight, this was my very first objective realization of just how isolated I was. It was weird and difficult, but because of Kathleen's warmth, knowledge and enthusiasm, I felt quite fearless—even eager—to explore within or without anything she asked me.

At the same time, true to my stubborn nature, in addition to not mentioning my shyness and childhood hurts, I held back on other things. For example, I didn't deem it necessary to tell her I'd dealt with problems through using alcohol because I no longer drank.

☙

At my fourth session, Kathleen surprised me by saying I'd have to go through maturation. She described it as the process people normally go through between the ages of eighteen and twenty-six and develop a greater awareness of the world and of themselves in it. This idea excited me enormously because I thought maybe Mother Nature had yet to provide me insight for well-being, something I'd missed out on during the normal period.

I agreed to become a student of adolescence and listened closely to her advice.

"Get more resources for yourself: buy books and take workshops. Read novels by authors such as Doris Lessing whose heroes experience growth during adolescence; take time out and meditate about life's stages and about life in general; look around you at how other people behave when they're talking; and especially, watch how your outgoing son, Conrad, behaves. And, Helen, keep a journal."

During my weekly appointments, I marveled at my therapist's knowledge of human behavior. I was amazed to learn my problems had existed all along, right there in books, analyzed many times by others. I listened, *really listened*, and took notes. I saw how much time I'd lost by not getting professional help earlier. I put as much energy as I could into my personal evolution to make sure that maturation worked for me this time.

Kathleen introduced me to the work of psychologists who were pioneering studies about the healthy individual. Richard Riso's *Personality Types* was based on the 2,500-year-old Chinese system of personality descriptions called the Enneagram. The book describes nine personality types, with healthy, average and unhealthy aspects of each one. Everyone has optimal aspects as well as undesirable ones. I learned that it wasn't just a few others and myself with personality problems, but that every single person in the world had to "manage" their behavior or else miss out on being a whole person.

I read sections of Riso's book over and over, trying to decide my type. At first I thought I was number 5, the Thinker, because I liked to examine my problems; then 9, the Peacemaker, because I hated to argue; then number 1, the Reformer, because I wanted change to happen; then 2, the Helper, because I often did things for others instead of doing what I needed for myself.

Although I longed to know my type, I refrained from asking Kathleen what it was. Some instinct in addition to my normal shyness held me back, telling me I wasn't ready to benefit from knowing it. About fifteen years later, I learned I was a 4, The Artist, and by then, after a lot of growing, I was mature enough to appreciate some of the idiosyncrasies of that type.

I didn't just read; I also meditated, as Kathleen suggested. I didn't necessarily "meditate," but I looked at ideas or people in ways I'd never considered and it made me feel a little brave. On one sunny day with new snow blanketing the ground, I parked my car in a place with a pretty view and sat quietly with my surroundings.

What, I thought, does it matter if I'm forty-two; at least I'm working on my growth. I wonder how I'll feel after I mature... Will I think differently? What should I think about today? I'll look at Ellen (the mother of Anthony's best friend). What does she do that I don't? A lot. She sure has her life well organized; she wears those colorful pants and irons her blouses. I never iron. She takes all three of her children to sports. She drives all the way to Boston just to have beauty treatments! She sure pays a lot of attention to herself. Yes, she's well organized. She also walks standing straight and speaks with such self-assurance. Could I be like her? What about her would I like to do?"

I didn't miss alcohol. In order to give it up, at cocktail time I did what I'd done to give up smoking: take walks, call someone, or engage in something completely self-sustaining, such as reading. Now, while with groups at church or the few parties we attended, I did something different and productive: I observed. It was still awkward to stand by myself, but by concentrating on the behavior of those around me the nagging awareness of being a social misfit lessened.

It surprised me to see warm facial expressions during simple informational exchanges. Next I discovered a world of nonverbal communications and saw that smiles occurring during them often appeared as heartwarming as the ones during conversations. I wanted some of that warmth, though I still didn't know how to get it.

Regardless of how inferior I might feel at social settings, during the drive home my family's warmth helped rebuild my self-assurance. Once home I felt fine unless I'd perceived someone had deliberately offended me. It took me a long, long time but eventually I realized that very few people purposely insulted me. Rather, because I'd been too shy to ask for clarification of what was said, I would misconstrue things. I continued to attend church on Sunday mornings because I knew in my heart that someday, somehow, I would feel good there.

At home, instead of drinking to alleviate stress, I read books about personalities, kept a journal and daydreamed more than usual. Kathleen said it was good to imagine myself in warm experiences, so I thought about situations in which life went the way I wanted it to go. For example, having friends who held me in esteem; having money to do exciting things such as traveling first class with interesting friends and having people look to me for leadership in times of stress. I don't daydream much now, if at all. I tend to keep active while I'm awake, but back then, by relieving me of tension, it seemed to be helpful.

I still felt uncomfortable with relatives on the few occasions I saw them. I was certain they didn't care much for me. I told Kathleen about their ignoring me during the summer after the fire, now four years ago, while I lived in the camper beside the ashes. That rankled me still.

"In all societies it's customary for neighbors to comfort each other in times of a disaster, and the fact that no one came to see you, to invite you over for lunch or for a cup of coffee to try to help, is strange." After thinking a bit she went on, "I believe they felt envy about your mother's close relationships with Aunt Llewellyn and Nana, and for that reason ignored your needs. In any case, don't waste time worrying about them because—at least for now—nothing good can come from it."

Instead, she encouraged me to develop skills, and, because I'd longed to sing since childhood, I sought a voice teacher. I asked the lead soprano from the UU church, who had taught for years, if she would give me lessons. She hesitated before saying she was too busy. I soon found out she accepted other new people. I wished I didn't have such an insignificant personality that sometimes put people off when I asked for something. Although I felt relief in many ways from Kathleen's help, I still felt very low on the social totem pole. I hadn't complained to her about my childhood, and her treatment for me focused on my present problems.

Consequently, the bulk of my childhood pain remained, loomed before me and I seldom left its shadow. I didn't know anyone else who gave lessons, so I had to wait to start singing.

When Kathleen suggested I not see her until after the tax season because I was too busy, I was horrified—but too shy to tell her. Today I think she might have helped me in many areas, including how to be a better parent, if she'd continued to counsel me on a regular basis instead of on and off. But I can only blame myself for this because I hadn't told her about old pain and I doubt she knew how much I hurt. I'd become pretty good at hiding my inner self.

ଓ

Like Prince Edward Island's sticky red dirt, residue from my upbringing permeated everything, including mothering my children.

I didn't see Anthony as Anthony. Although his report cards showed him to be a B+ student, I saw him as brilliant. I was determined he would find great success and not face the problems I had while growing up.

I built hopes he would become a doctor—I loved the sound of Dr. Anthony Rivas. Being the fourth generation, he would be Dr. Anthony Rivas the Fourth and I knew his family in Venezuela would be happy, too. All of this was based on his interest in animals and nature. I just assumed he would find a profession in the sciences and didn't suggest he explore other fields.

Now I see communing with nature was natural for him because it was right there in his backyard, but that that didn't mean he wanted science for a profession. I too had found relief from social pressures in the outdoors, both in Cos Cob and in P.E.I., but it didn't occur to me that this was what my son was doing.

Anthony was kind and patient with people as well as with animals, and though he had few friends, they were constant, so it never occurred to me he lacked social skills. If I'd been alert to Anthony's teachers, I might have caught my shortsightedness earlier.

When he was fourteen, Kennebunk High selected Anthony as a recipient of a full scholarship to attend a three-week Outward Bound course on Hurricane Island, off the coast of Maine. I questioned at the time why he was chosen to go—why Anthony who lived in one of the beautiful homes at Crescent Surf and not some child with fewer opportunities. But I didn't seriously look into it. Now, I think Anthony's teachers saw him as someone who could benefit in what Outward Bound prided itself on—building self-confidence.

He returned from the course awash in a glow of self-assurance. He gave me a bear hug, smiling from ear to ear. "Mom, you wouldn't believe it! Every day twelve of us, boys and girls, rowed everywhere and around the Island. We slept on long oars laid lengthwise over the crossbows at night in a boat specially designed for Outward Bound by a man from Kennebunk. It's like the boats the Vikings used; we could both sail it and row it. We'd get up at six and splash into the water. You wouldn't believe how cold it was! We all went to the bathroom sitting on the edge of the boat."

He couldn't stop talking about it.

"Each of us spent a three-day solo on a tiny island with few provisions, including a little bag of nuts. We had to forage around for food, water and stuff to build a shelter to sleep in.

They gave us a pad and pencil to write down our thoughts. We also did tree climbing where we had to trust our partner on the ground to hold us safely with ropes while we swung in the air twenty feet up."

How surprised I was to see the change in him. I had a glimpse of a life without anguish and anxiety, but because we didn't talk more about his experience and build on those good feelings, somehow they disappeared in the everyday shuffle of happenings.

Because I was unfamiliar with such happy feelings, I couldn't process them. I even lacked the vocabulary to discuss them, so I wound up blanking it out of my mind, as was my usual tendency concerning unpleasant thoughts.

Now I ask myself if there were other reasons why I didn't encourage Anthony to build upon his great experience. Did I feel resentment that I hadn't been given more understanding and love from my parents when I was a child? Was it because I lacked a role model for achieving self-growth when I was growing up? I suspect a combination of these factors paralyzed my emotions and therefore my actions, causing me to "refuse" to give love and encouragement to my children on certain occasions.

Conrad, on the other hand, always had many friends and a variety of activities. Once I drove him to rehearsals for a community production of *Oliver*, about fifteen miles away. During three hours, three days a week, for six weeks, I usually stayed and watched for two reasons: I didn't want to do the long drive twice and because Kathleen had advised me to observe this son, to learn from him how to be more outgoing.

My younger son got along with everyone. Sometimes during breaks, he meandered around the stage walking on his hands, with absolutely no self-consciousness, with almost as much ease as he walked on his feet. I couldn't believe my eyes! How did I get to have a child like that?

I felt I had no worries about his future because he didn't suffer from any of my weaknesses. That there were other things a person could suffer from didn't occur to me. He performed in a play at Kennebunk High that fall and participated in several sports. His participation in sports intrigued me: I couldn't begin to fathom how it would feel to box and hit someone or to wrestle and squeeze my arms around people.

ઌ

Roland made me feel good in many ways. When issues concerning others confused me, I would go talk to him. He usually agreed with my point of view and would say something like, "Forget it, it's not important," especially if it had to do with my relatives. He anticipated my needs, such as organizing the shopping, preparing for guests, and registering my car. He did so much thinking for me, he almost ran my life. And I really appreciated it, because I lacked many of the skills to do it myself.

He added several pleasing personal touches as well, such as placing photographs of us on his dresser and giving me gifts of my favorite things, such as a plaque in the shape of a goose to hang keys on. He often had something for me on Mother's Day, on Valentine's, as well as Christmas. He made me feel important in front of others when he said things such as "Helen knows; ask Helen" or "Helen keeps track of things."

I liked his physical proximity, too. I snuggled beside him when we watched television at night during the national network news, the *McNeil Lehrer News Hour* and especially during dramatic serial shows like *Dallas*. When we walked on our beach, on Kennebunk Beach or on a sidewalk, either he took my hand or I took his arm and we moved in unison. He was my hero, my "King," I teased him.

But Roland still didn't respond to my awkwardly presented worries about personal growth problems. To my dismay, the knot of pain hidden so deep inside remained inviolate because I couldn't describe it in a way that made sense, not even to myself. My thoughts just got jumbled up, I presume from the troubled emotions encasing them.

On the few occasions when I tried to talk about it, Roland took over the conversation with thoughts about his own upbringing. Silenced by his monologue and frustrated by being tongue-tied, at those moments I felt more like a silent partner than a participant.

When I got angry with Roland, I was unable to express it with satisfaction. Being shy, I had not often articulated anger and what I said when angry often didn't make sense, so Roland would ignore it. This left the nature of my anger in partial obscurity, and instead of getting relief, I felt added frustration.

☙

Nat called on Friday night, March 9, 1985. "I'm sorry to have to tell you this, Helen, but Dad died last night in his sleep. He'll be buried in the British Cemetery in the same plot as Mom. Can you come?"

A jumble of sad emotions from the loss of our father flung me into painful memories of my childhood and stopped my mind from functioning rationally. All I could think about was the deep snow and freezing cold temperatures that made it hard just to get up to Kennebunk, so how could I fly to Portugal for a weekend and be back to help with business early the following week? All I said was I couldn't make it, that there wasn't enough time. Nat didn't say much more.

Other than my mother's brief funeral behind the British Hospital in Lisbon, we've had no shared family affairs–no weddings or graduations with family present. The only family occasions were Christmas and Thanksgiving, and we didn't even celebrate Thanksgiving after we moved to Canada. We didn't have any family gatherings during the two years I'd lived in Portugal. I don't feel like starting now when both my parents are gone.

I burrowed into tax preparation. My life went on as usual except, in the quiet of the night, tears fell on my pillow when I thought of the last time I saw my father–his fine white hair no longer covering the top of his head and deep furrows running across his brow. I saw the whites of his eyes and enlarged pupils dwarfing his now blurry, hazel brown irises. His cheeks sagged and he was only as tall as I. Although he'd started to use a cane, he moved around the large, five-star hotel lobby faster than ever.

His mind worked proficiently, too. More than once he said, "Be happy with your life, enjoy your friends, nature and animals. Stay out of the rat-race to make money." Or, "The farm is beautiful; with a little care you can bring the old apple trees back to life and raise bees for honey." Up to the end of his ninety-three years, he loved the simple life more than anything.

☙

I wanted to mature because I was sure it would help me lead a more serene and fulfilling life. Soon after the tax season in 1985, I restarted my concentration on growing up.

I had the perfect place for it, a recent addition to our house that we called the Old Garage. We had moved the second floor of an old building in the woods, where it had been vacant since the 1910s. A stableman and later a chauffeur had lived on the upper floor. The first floor was too rotted to be moved.

I wanted this building to connect me with the past that I'd lost when my house burned. The odor of the old wood reminded me of my grandmother's and aunt's houses, which had been built at about the same time. I set up a chair and table in a portion of the Old Garage where I meditated, read and made notes. A window, a few feet behind my chair provided light, and an interior wall framed the front of my table. Nothing else but an old zinc bathtub occupied the space.

Sitting quietly, I let the atmosphere sink in. The wood worked: it stirred up memories of Nana and Aunt Llewellyn, allowing me to feel peaceful and relaxed. I felt rather like a young girl, happy with her own special place, eager to grow.

For days, while spring worked wonders outdoors, my unusual surroundings caused me to work my mind. I contemplated the evolution of history: Were we getting anywhere since Aunt Llewellyn's inquiries into human nature? I doubted it; no person or government had figured out how to run the world and how could we ever have world peace without that? I pondered the irresistible dilemma of which came first, the chicken or the egg, until I got dizzy. I asked myself if something as basic as that had no known answer, did anything?

There was no telephone, the children were at school, and Roland worked uptown at payroll. I had all day, all week and no demands to accomplish anything. Each day I walked and sat, and sat and walked around the gray-brown rooms with boards for floors and walls. I opened and closed my eyes, all the while stretching my mind with other abstract questions, such as what is the human race, and why is it so hard to have meaningful, caring societies?

One mid-May sunny Monday morning, instead of sitting and walking around, I remained at my table. I stared at the ceiling made from unpainted, tongue-in-grove narrow boards. I focused on their acquired reddish-tan hues, abundantly adorned with mottled gray designs of varying sizes and shapes. Many of them seemed to be distorted faces with untamed hair.

And then all at once, as if from nearby, a clear, strong voice startled me into attention. In essence, it assured me I was connected to every single person in the whole world by a universal network of love. Feelings of belonging, warmth and joy strummed through me. I felt the impact of love.

When the effect lessened, it flashed through my mind I wouldn't mind dying because I'd experienced the wonder and glory of love—I knew nothing would ever be more important than that. My second thought, a sad one, was that neither my mother nor some of her cousins had reached this state.

My third and last immediate thought was, *No way do I want to die!* The world had opened for me. There are people to meet, to know, to love! I vowed at that moment to be careful with my life and to live it to the fullest.

With extra care I stood and moved my limbs, because it felt as if I'd abandoned them for a while. I collected my thoughts to see if they were real. Yes, I was the same person, but yes, I was changed. I'd acquired the precious link to the outside world and I felt much, much more like a complete human being.

But—the energy had even more to teach me. A little later when my thoughts roamed to something about charity, I heard the voice again, softer this time. It gave the definition for the word *charity*. It sounded like an audiocassette that played in just exactly the same speed and tone as someone would read from a dictionary. As well as I can recall, it said something like, "Charity is not merely giving away things. It consists of love and forgiveness for others, plus a strong feeling within yourself for wanting to help others, in order to create a fairer, kinder world."

Within a day, speaking with the same deliberation, the voice revealed several more definitions for more value-related concepts such as honesty, love and truth. Each day, each week, I heard fewer definitions until, after six months, there were none.

Upon first examination, it's hard to understand that such phenomenal happenings didn't spur me right on to higher thoughts. I would like to be able to say that this changed my life, that I became a wiser, more thoughtful and caring person and that I joined philosophy discussion groups.

But I cannot. After all, without a doubt, my most critical need was to have a close friend. I craved warmth and understanding from a peer far more urgently than an intellectual outlook of the world.

Nevertheless, the definitions were not in vain. I heard them, but it took time to truly understand them and work them into my outlook. For example, in a couple of years I saw clearly why Christ had said that charity was one of the three most important virtues–I'd previously wondered why charity, if it merely meant giving things away, had been on Christ's shortlist of virtues.

Heartwarming though it was to know I was a part of universal love, with my timidity and ignorance of people I could not build on that principle and become more outgoing. However, following being given these insights I did fight harder with myself to overcome my social shortcomings.

I don't think anyone noticed changes in my behavior, and of course I was too timid to talk about these esoteric experiences, including my epiphany, even with Kathleen, who had advised me to meditate. I wouldn't talk about myself or anything unless someone asked me specific questions, and although we had lunch together from time to time and took courses later on at Harvard, Kathleen no longer "counseled" me.

9

Revisiting My Adolescence

With the insights gained from meditation I not only felt an urgency to embrace my new life but, especially at first, to be the teenager I never was. One day, in spring of 1985, I rode my children's motorbike five miles, up to Kennebunk. (They were allowed to use it only on our property.) I was so determined to make the trip I overrode my dread of seeing someone who might know me. I leaned backwards and forwards over the handlebars the way I imagined a seasoned rider might, all the while singing Elvis Presley songs and breathing in great gobs of air.

I had complained of sore feet to Kathleen a year earlier, and she recommended, "Wear Birkenstocks!" Now I bought some of these odd sandals, the aches disappeared, and she complimented me: "You're moving up."

Next I got my ears pierced. Now I could buy those odd assemblages of feathers, beads and glass that dangled from the ears and swung from the necks of hippie women. Well, I didn't go that far–in actuality, I only bought earrings of a more classic design. But to get my ears pierced was an important ritual.

After having searched for a year, I finally found an elderly Christ's Church choir member who gave singing lessons, and he agreed to teach me. I was apprehensive because I had never before enrolled in private lessons—and because so much hurt was connected with music. It reminded me of my sad days in Cos Cob when I was shut in my room during musical soirees and of my failed attempts to learn to play the piano.

My first session was as awkward as anything in my whole life. With no chair or table for support, with no accompaniment, I had to stand in the center of a strange room and sing from a bel canto exercise primer with a person I barely knew watching me. I gasped a little from time to time and barely refrained from crying. As soon as I drove away I broke down. But before I got home, blending in with tears from the past were tears of joy over my triumph of daring to sing!

I took lessons for ten weeks and then in place of classes my teacher invited me to join his church choir, which I promptly did. I cherished this activity with all my heart; not only did I enjoy singing beautiful music, but I also felt brave and forward moving.

Although it was 1985 and I was now forty-three years old, I felt like a teenager. I'd always wanted a swimming pool, so with adolescent determination I unleashed the verve and money to have one installed. It was, perhaps, the greatest symbol of my growth and I swam in it whenever the weather and my schedule cooperated. Anthony and Conrad liked it too, and Roland volunteered to be the pool caretaker.

After seeing Kathleen for a few sessions in the summer, she surprised me with an invitation. "I want to take a course on writing at Harvard next summer. Do you want to see what's available in the spring, and we can drive down there together? I could drive one week and you the other."

"Yes, sounds good," I said." But I was perplexed. *Does Kathleen want to be a friend? Why me, a patient? Wouldn't she have regular friends to drive down to Boston with...? Anyway, I'm looking forward to it.*

ଓ

That fall, in spite of engaging in stimulating activities to satisfy my "adolescence," emotional anxiety and stressful relationships at Crescent Surf remained oppressive. I no longer meditated. The cerebral element of my epiphany, the words that encouraged me to think about abstract concepts such as charity, conscience and forgiveness didn't interest me. I still had no friend with whom I could feel natural or genuine, and thus no one with whom I could share my sad past.

My relationship with my relatives veered onto an almost irreparable path. Almost two years after we'd begun plans for a subdivision, all of them ganged up at a Town Hall meeting to oppose its approval. Roland and I sat on the right in the hall and about twenty cousins on the left. The place was packed and the whole town witnessed my problems. I stared at my lap and thought about my wretched situation: I was losing the ability to be comfortable in the one place in the world where I wanted to enjoy my roots–the place where my grandmother and aunt had given me safe haven.

When the town sided with our lawyer on most of the provisions for our development, Roland nudged me and conveyed with a smile, "We won." Little did he know, regardless of what the town did, I was devastated.

The rift pained me every single day, especially when I had to drive past cousins' houses to go to town. I didn't turn to Roland because he would merely reiterate, "Let's move away," and I didn't want to bother Kathleen about it because I thought I'd complained enough to her about my relatives.

To try to lighten my stress, I decided to read. At the summer library sale I picked up a blue hardcover book with no jacket by Taylor Caldwell. I'd enjoyed a novel by her when I lived at my parents' in Portugal and, not even opening it, bought it for a dollar.

A few days later, on a gray afternoon, I curled up on a faded green velvet wingback chair with the blue book and noticed the title, *The Turnbulls,* published in 1943. I quickly recognized it was a saga about generations of family feuding, about insidious and destructive consequences caused by hatred and vindictiveness. My heart climbed into my throat while I read each page in the whole book with horror. I couldn't believe I'd randomly bought a book that exemplified the type of family relationships I, and to some extent, my parents, suffered at Crescent Surf. Hatred, that ugly feeling, churning away at my gut, caused the Turnbulls to annihilate one another, and I realized I had to do something fast.

So that night, before sleeping, I sat in a cross-legged yoga position, determined to find an answer to this so I didn't feel hatred. I sat like that for a while and pondered solutions, but everything seemed so complicated. That night I dreamed I was standing on my property near Lily Pond, a marshy area, and it was jammed full of big turtles and small ones. My relatives floundered in the same pond, screaming, sinking, their arms flailing wildly as they battled the turtles to gain a grip on the few rocks.

A thunderous voice from the woods called to me, "What should we do, save the relatives or the turtles?" With little hesitation I boomed back, "Let the turtles keep their stones." I felt powerful in this dream, and not in the least remorseful about "eliminating" my relatives.

When I ran into Kathleen uptown a few days later, I poured out the story of the turtle dream. With her eyes wide opened, she grabbed hold of my arm. "Helen, that was evil working in you! But that's good, because only through understanding evil will you learn goodness."

At first I doubted it was evil, but didn't say anything. At home I questioned myself about the nature of evil and realized I knew next to nothing about it. However, the effects of the dream did lessen my anxiety for a few years, and by then, I was learning how to deal with hatred in a healthier way.

☙

That winter, 1986, McGill University accepted Anthony into their biology program. With some remorse, I realized I hadn't much time left to be a good mother for him. I knew I would never stop missing him, and as a farewell gesture, I decided to do something special with him as part of his graduation ritual. Because he was going to Canada to study, it seemed appropriate to take a trip to Prince Edward Island and show him where I grew up. He agreed, and we left in early June.

Nothing much had changed in the Maritimes; it even seemed about as desolate as when I'd driven through with my mother en route to visit Nana in the fifties. It was a long drive and Anthony listened to ***The Best of Dire Straits***, some of his favorite music.

As we passed by our former house on the Island, I slowed down, felt horrible and pointed it out at the top of the long lane, the lane that reminded me of isolation, bleakness, loneliness. My throat narrowed and I couldn't talk. I drove on. Although in a way I was eager to discuss my life on the farm, I couldn't get up the courage to explain how I'd suffered there. Anthony must have sensed my anguish for he didn't ask to see the house any closer.

Most of the Island–rolling low green hills, plowed fields and tiny villages–offered as little excitement for Anthony as it had for me when I was a teenager. "Whew!" he commiserated after four days, "I can see you lived a boring life up here!" I felt good that Anthony knew something about my past, even if lingering misery was keeping me silent about it.

Conrad, now fifteen, worked at Cape Able bicycle shop in Kennebunkport and hung out with friends. At home he tended to talk on the telephone or stay in his room where he read all of Carlos Castaneda's series about the teachings the author claimed to have received from a Mexican shaman. I browsed through the books, didn't believe in the author's professed contacts with supernatural entities, and had little to discuss with him about it.

He had taken up cycling, and Roland and I drove him to races once or twice a month, at first in Kennebunk, and then to places farther away. My heart thrilled to see my son win so often! In Fitchburg, Massachusetts, where Conrad won his section, I stood there smiling, but he didn't share his triumph by looking in my direction, at least not right away, and a little something within me cringed.

Then, soon after competing unsuccessfully in the Olympic youth trials in Plattsburg, New York, he stopped racing without talking about it. Finally I asked why he no longer raced, "Mom, I can't compete without belonging to a team, and the closest ones are in Boston. The guys get free equipment and coaching. A rider can't do it alone unless they have money."

I wished he'd shared more with me about his decision to give up the sport that had been a cornerstone of his life for a couple of years. Then again, I hadn't set good examples of conveying personal matters. I wondered, with chagrin, if he resented the fact we didn't have more money.

ର

Kathleen and I decided which courses we would take at Harvard Summer School in 1986. I was interested in writing—I don't know where the dream to write came from and I hardly expected it to materialize. She chose creative writing, and I expository writing, because the former had never appealed to me.

But I was even more excited over doing something with a peer. This would be my first time doing something on a grand scale with one, and it was going to last for ten weeks!

Kathleen discussed aspects of her life every single time we made the three-hour drive to and from Cambridge. Born in London during the war, she was three when sirens sounded overhead and her mother rushed her underground with a paper bag over her head so she "wouldn't get scared." Later her parents sent her and her two older sisters to live in the countryside with relatives. There she learned that her father, a medical doctor, and her mother, had separated.

As a teenager, she experienced stressful times with her mother and two sisters after they moved to New York City. She married a millionaire and after six years of living together in a wealthy suburb, divorced. Then she married and divorced a professor of sociology at the University of Orono, Maine. Later she obtained a doctorate in psychology at San Diego. She kept me spellbound and her stories kindled desires to express ideas of my own.

She talks about her hurts and pains like she'd describe anything she didn't like—a book or a movie. I can't say a word about what bothers me. She's so different. Will I ever be like that?

For sure, many times during the car trips I would have liked to talk about myself, about my problems—especially about my big difficulty with shyness—but my inability to speak about personal things—even about my epiphany—kept me silent. During a lull I thought that Kathleen was opening my eyes to other people. I had never heard a woman reveal so much of her life and it fascinated me. I realize now that I was putting the principles of being objective into practice, maybe for one of the first times. I did this by seeing Kathleen in different contexts, in different places with a variety of influences affecting her. Usually I saw people only in the circumstances of the present.

ଔ

I had never known he could paint. I didn't think of him as an artist. He was my spouse whom I knew intimately and whom I thought of as doing many things—such as operating computers, interpreting I.R.S. manuals and reviewing the architectural plans for our new home. But after the 1987 income tax season, Roland painted almost daily in the upstairs of our office. I liked his work. He did colorful, bold drawings of strange heads and a few landscapes of pine trees.

For the first time I saw how focused Roland could be. He was so very quiet that sometimes I felt he didn't care about me. Something I read in Shakespeare at university said that silence and secrecy were akin, and Roland's aloofness bred contempt and suspicion, but I tried to ignore these distressing thoughts.

When I complained about the silence, he would respond, "That's the way I am; I can't do anything about it." I thought to myself he didn't try to change. I was quite happy when we were doing things together, like working or going on a trip, but when I thought about his having something else that was as important or more so than I was, I questioned our relationship. Roland did fulfill my need for detail about what he was doing when I pressed for an answer, so I usually wound up feeling all right about it. However, he didn't say what most women want to hear from their spouses: I love you more than anything else.

He was my engine, though, and I needed him. He still organized my life and without him I wouldn't know where to go or what to do. He was my big love; he came before anything else in my life, and I wished I knew he felt the same way about me.

Then one evening I looked at him objectively. He was stretched out on the couch, his head propped at a right angle by an oddly folded pillow. One hand was suspended in the air and the other held a book. Seeing him that way, I realized Roland really knew how to relax. One of my major goals was to learn to do that and here I had an exemplary model right in front of me.

Nothing upsets him, not the house burning down or having little money. Anthony's about to go to McGill. What would I do if he weren't Canadian and I had to pay more than a token tuition! And what if he didn't have his father to live with in Montreal? But everything's working out and I shouldn't get upset. I'll try harder to relax myself.

In the fall, when lodging rates were low, Roland planned a five-day trip for us at Monhegan Island, an artists' retreat, to learn what artists were doing there. A small, open motorboat carried mail and about five passengers for nine miles on the Atlantic to a little cove and a tiny, pine-dotted, rocky outcropping.

There were no roads or cars: just a few tourists sampling the simple life by strolling on animal-made paths. Artists lived in rented studios. We stayed at one of the two large but plain hotels and ate self-serve at communal tables.

At our very first meal, Roland and two women artists from New York City sitting next to us dove into an extraordinary, lively discussion about art.

He never bubbles away like this with me. I'd never seen him so outgoing before. I'm so ignored, as ignored as ever I've been during my whole life, and I haven't any idea what I can say in this group.

I sat stiff as a board on my hard wooden bench and watched the three of them chat like old friends. As soon as we left the dining room, I exploded. "You didn't look at me at all; I may as well have been eating all by myself!"

"That's not true. It's all in your head." Roland had a knack for pretending situations didn't happen. Regardless of whether it existed just in my head or not, his curt response didn't ease my hurt. Stung by jealousy, I semi-sulked during the remaining four days on Monhegan. Although we didn't eat with those two artists again, foggy, wet weather set in, and every night the foghorns, anchored next to us, wailed incessantly, their forlorn sound echoing my discontent.

Following this trip, fear of invoking jealousy made me steer us away from certain types of social events, thereby impeding the social development I had begun. I was Roland's partner, my life revolved around his, so I did everything to keep him by my side.

ꟹ

In ten years our income tax business had grown five hundred percent. We hired employees, but I worked too much, and in 1988 a disturbing throb appeared above my right temple. Kathleen told me to pay attention to it. Two new clients informed me that their prior tax professionals had died from heart-related problems, preparers in their late forties, not unlike me.

In February, for a break, when skies were deep blue and splashes of sunlight twinkled everywhere on crusty snow, I read Shirley MacLaine's book, *Out on a Limb*. I'd never been exactly sure what the word *flamboyant* meant, but I decided

Out on a Limb qualified. MacLaine claimed while living in a tent with no heat in the snowy Andean mountains, a single serape, made out of wool from llamas, sufficed to keep her warm.

But that was just the beginning of her experiences: spirits visited her in her tent and showered her with profound insight on how to achieve the supreme life. I wanted to be flamboyant, too. In hindsight, I guess I already was in the sense that an unknown voice had urged me to develop too—but I didn't think of this similarity at that time, perhaps because MacLaine could talk about her personal life and I could not.

My voice within, the one that may have worked in tandem with the one in my revelation, kept urging me to try something new, especially to work with people. It had been three years since my epiphany, and the important constructs for building a personal philosophy and feeling connected with others remained largely untapped.

Then our oldest employee agreed to buy our tax business. We calculated that the money from the sale would support us for five years, enough time, we thought, to find another source of income.

In order to satisfy my new drive to explore ideas with people, and at the same time fulfill my old wish to study history, that summer I enrolled in the graduate department at the University of New Hampshire, located fifty minutes away. With a doctorate, I envisioned myself in scintillating discussions.

I selected a course in Middle East History to build on what I'd learned in Granada, Spain, where for three months I'd studied Islamism and Arabic. I loved my new freedom to use my mind. I set up a study in the Old Garage, now pretty well furnished, but still rustic and smelling of the old wood.

Shortly, my professor asked me to write a review of *Migration to the North*, by Tayyeh Salih, a Sudanese author.

I noted in Salih's foreword that he wrote his novel during the wee hours of the morning while in a state of semi-unconsciousness. So, I thought, if I get up in the very early morning to read it, maybe my mind will be in the same condition and I'll be better able to understand his thoughts. It worked: his stories and theories became alive.

The professor was pleased. "Your paper tops what I've seen so far in the international journals; most reviewers get bogged down with the author's obscure symbolism. You write well, and your ideas are intelligent." I was elated to know I could write good essays. I attributed my success–my comprehension–to getting up early, though I was too timid to explain this phenomenon to the professor.

After one semester, I realized it would take many years to prepare myself for teaching at university and I didn't want to wait so long to work with people.

Roland, too, wanted change. Propelled by Joseph Campbell's six-part televised series about spiritual development, especially his suggestion to "follow your bliss," he decided to paint full-time. With money his father provided, he rented a gigantic loft in an otherwise unused old brick building in the largely abandoned waterfront in Portland.

No longer studying, I went to his loft frequently to see his paintings. On one such visit in November, Roland stopped painting, washed his hands and took my hand. "Let's sit down and talk over some ideas I've been thinking about."

We sat on a couple of semi-dilapidated chairs he'd picked up from the street. "You know, Portland doesn't have a place for artists who aren't known or for ones who are experimenting. I've got the paperwork from my former consultant projects and I can use it to set up a nonprofit, tax-exempt organization. That way, we can raise money to run the gallery from grants; it won't be able to pay you anything at first, but will you manage it?"

"But," I stammered, staring at him, "I don't know anything about art. Or artists!"

"As manager," he said, "you don't need to worry about that. Besides, I'll help when necessary. You'll learn as we go along. Think about it and we can talk more later."

I drove home deep in thought. I *can't believe Roland's offering me just what I need: to work with people. I never even told him how much I wanted that. Let's see, for starters, next time Kathleen and I go to Harvard, I'll take a course on art. What a change!...*

But what will it be like to be with artists? I don't do well talking with regular people. I can't envision talking with artists. Roland will guide me though and I trust him. Besides, I'll be in Portland and we can go to movies, theaters and restaurants. It will take me away from Crescent Surf for most of the week.... I'll be with people. Yes, definitely, I'll do it!

In the beginning there was little for me to do while Roland was in the process of erecting walls. He loved his huge space, and strode around its openness as if he'd taken full ownership. One day he showed me his recent paintings and soon asked, "What's Conrad doing when school's over?"

"Oh, he'll probably go to Montreal to study."

"Well, Helen, that means we don't have to stay here in the winter now. Wouldn't it be nice to go to someplace warm? The gallery doesn't need to be open all year." It seemed strange for me to think about going someplace else, but without my children at home, everything was different and I didn't like long cold winters, either. "Sounds good."

Soon after that conversation, we saw a two-page article in the *New York Times* about San Miguel de Allende, describing it as an artists' haven in central Mexico. Roland said, "Hmm, this might be a place for us to go. Let's check it out. Maybe Mort"—an acquaintance from church who drove to Mexico every year—"knows about it."

I'd love to be in a Latino culture again! Spain was so wonderful—all the sun, music and flashing brown eyes. This time I wouldn't be by myself—I'd be with Roland and wouldn't have to worry about being timid. He's got great ideas. I never would have thought of going to Mexico, even though it's right beside the United States. Mom used to send me all those postcards with colorful bougainvillea and Mayan pyramids. I can't wait to go!

That Sunday after the service, we spoke with Mort about San Miguel de Allende. He said he knew little about it but would introduce us to Royal and Nancy who'd spent a whole winter there.

Nancy and Royal came to visit the next Sunday, and because many people get lost trying to find our place, we were on the lookout for them. On time and not lost, they edged around the top of our lane in a long navy blue Cadillac, one with fins that dated back at least a dozen years. The license plate read UU 1. With considerable deliberation,

Royal slid all six-foot-two of his large frame from the automobile, while Nancy debarked with a bounce and wide smile.

Nancy, about my height and several years older, wore a pretty lavender cape. "Royal had it made for me," she explained when I commented on it, "and I almost always wear it." She was especially well read and versed in philosophy and religions, but she didn't talk to show her erudition; rather she responded to my questions to help me understand her life and to be of assistance by sharing her knowledge of Mexico. I didn't feel at all shy with her.

Royal's alert blue eyes contrasted pleasantly with his tan pallor. His stature and conservative dress commanded attention, his measured diction respect. Although he didn't speak often, when he did, his voice was so low I had to sit on the edge of my chair in order to hear.

"I just retired from the Boston Center for the Arts, where I was its Founder and President for eighteen years. At the same time, I did some work and spent many hours volunteering at the Unitarian headquarters on Beacon Hill."

Roland piped up, in response, "I'm starting a nonprofit alternative artists gallery in Portland. Helen's agreed to be the manager. I want to set up an advisory board that would consist of artists and arts professionals. Would you be interested?" Royal said sure, he'd like to be involved.

When they left, they insisted we stay with them when we went to Mexico, and we made plans for April. I was mesmerized we were doing so much together. I'd never socialized with anyone as knowledgeable and so friendly. My new life was blossoming. I was so excited.

Named after the street it was on, Danforth Gallery needed to become known in Portland, but we didn't know anyone in the Portland art community. As president of the gallery, a nonprofit, tax-exempt artists' space, Roland could not profit from showing his paintings in it, and all he had to attract attention to the gallery was his art. So we planned an exhibition of it and, to reconcile the need not to be self-serving, if any works were to sell, all the money would go to the gallery.

I advertised as best I could, inviting the public to the opening night of a new gallery to see an exhibition of paintings called "Roland's Friends," by Salazar . Roland had decided to use his middle name, Salazar, as his artist's name because he liked its uniqueness. He'd been christened with this name after a Mexican friend of his father.

In preparation, Roland and I cut up cheese for refreshments, not speaking, and silently dreading no one would show up. Not only were we unknown, in an abandoned neighborhood, but also it was four below zero outside!

Wearing my warmest clothing, I was shivering in the unheated gallery when Royal and Nancy arrived. Shortly, the gallery brimmed with curious and determined art lovers who walked up the two flights of stairs in the Old Molasses Building, so named because clipper ships from the Caribbean had deposited molasses in it during the nineteenth century.

I was so cold and in surroundings so weird it seemed out of place to feel shy. I could see nothing but centuries-old brick walls, warped wooden flooring and artsy people wearing long coats and colorful scarves. *Flamboyant* types, that's what they were. I smiled, enjoying the word. The viewers stayed a couple of hours eating cheese, drinking wine, talking–and looking at each painting.

Because without a doubt, what spun the opening like a top, was Roland's art. Even I was staggered by the impact of his work hanging on all the walls under spotlights. Many of the thirty works on canvas were huge, measuring eight feet by four feet. Drawn with brown and red Conté crayon and shaded with pale yellows, blues and orange-red paints, some contained large, semi-abstract, eccentric bald heads with riveting and piercing eyes. In one, figures in a boat, dressed as clergy, appeared to discuss religion; in another, figures adorned as rich people sat at a large table and divvied up food in a stingy fashion. Some of his "friend" protagonists stood in groups of twos and threes with frightened grimaces looking out over a fence half-hidden in green leafy trees. Another painting depicted a nuclear summer with only remnants of people. Some of their bodies had few limbs and other limbs had partially melted.

My sixty-year-old spouse had revealed his soul for the first time.

The viewers and a statewide critic applauded the art, and during the six weeks the show was up, four talented arts-related individuals joined Royal, Roland and me on the Advisory Board of Directors. We became Portland's first and only nonprofit, tax-exempt, alternative artists' gallery. Nothing sold; we derived no money. We didn't plan to reopen to the public until July to allow time to organize when we returned from Mexico.

10

A Year of Major Change

On April 18, 1989, Roland and I flew to Mexico City en route to Royal and Nancy's. On the plane we reread Royal's two-page letter, written on airmail paper with little holes made by his typewriter. It detailed advice for how to travel, where to stay and what to see and eat en route. Accordingly, at the historic Majestic Hotel, we took an exterior room on the fourth floor that overlooked the Zócalo, one of the world's largest plazas, bordered by old, ornate, government buildings, hundreds of precious metal shops and a sagging cathedral.

As foretold by Royal, bugles playing taps woke us at 5:30. Bleary-eyed, we stood on our balcony and watched a couple dozen soldiers unfurl and raise with precision-like movements a huge red, white and green flag with a sprawling copper-colored eagle and a snake squiggling from its mouth. There was no going back to sleep.

I was as enthralled by history as when I'd first visited the Puerta del Sol in Madrid, back in 1962, but now my life was much improved. I had my spouse with me, and timidity didn't preoccupy me as it had then. I was here to enjoy!

Feeling like ants, we walked across the Zócalo. In the main patio at the National Palace, larger-than-life murals by Diego Rivera showed Spaniards mutilating and killing natives. At the time I felt compassion, but today it makes me think of the equivalent art being shown in the Capital Rotunda in Washington, displaying our soldiers slaughtering American Indians, and I know that isn't likely to happen.

For the rest of the day we visited several art museums and galleries. Roland's guiding hand and keen eye helped me appreciate various technical and aesthetic artistic values.

The next day, following Royal's suggestion, we left for San Miguel de Allende on the Blue Train. While I looked out the window at hilly gullies and cactus plants, I felt blessed with how rewarding the trip had been so far. The details Royal had given us were making all the difference. What a difference to have friends.

ꝏ

Fine-grained light-pink dust colored the small train station in San Miguel, as if it were an Impressionist painting. We got into a shiny lime green and white taxi, and, going just a little faster than some burros by our side, made our way over hole-ridden, narrow cobblestone streets, bordered by shops hanging their colorful ware outside. In the center of town we saw a tall pink cathedral, reminding me of a children's book. Roland and I looked knowingly at each other; we were going to love this.

Our friends greeted us with an eagerness to show us their treasured winter lifestyle. Nancy seemed even more jovial and relaxed than I'd remembered her being in Maine. While she prepared supper, she told me about living in San Miguel.

"You can eat anything, but stay away from the strawberries, and always wash the lettuce and afterward soak it in water with iodine drops. Make sure you wash your hands every time you come home, especially when you touch money, and never eat the street food, because the cooks at the stands don't have running water. Come shopping with me tomorrow, and I'll show you where I buy everything: the drugstore with discounted prices and the market stalls where I now trust some vendors. We just love it here, and I'm sure you and Roland will, too."

She's so kind. She's sort of like Nana, looking after me. I feel welcome and at home with her.

"Come with us this Sunday to our Unitarian Universalist Fellowship," Nancy said, drying her hands and sitting down with me. "It's not called a church, because we have no money for a minister. Royal is the chairperson; he does much of the planning and presides on Sundays. He'll probably ask you if you want to do a reading some Sunday once you get settled."

Could I really ever do that? I'd love to, but could I keep my hands from shaking and my voice from trembling? I know I won't be able to sleep for several nights before and that would make me look terrible, too. Just thinking about it makes my palms wet. Yet the idea thrills me, because if I can be brave enough to do it, then maybe my self-confidence will grow, and that will help me talk with people. How I want to have women friends my age, but out of shyness and lack of self-composure, I still can't be genuine with peers.

After two weeks of enjoying the beauty, warmth and relaxed atmosphere, after attending several concerts, art exhibitions and activities at the U.U. Fellowship, we decided to find a place to live for the next winter.

It took ten days, but we found a house just two days before we had to return. On a steep hill and up two flights of stairs, the early nineteenth-century sculpted wooden door with a brass owl knocker opened into a tastefully furnished condo.

In the kitchen antique-looking blue and white tiles covered just about everything. From the balcony I looked out over the whole town, a narrow lake and, in the distance, a mountain range. My insides somersaulted. I wouldn't have to worry about doing a thing to improve it. It had beauty, color, light, comfort, and even a maid. I couldn't wait to live here. I rushed across town to the owner with a check for four hundred dollars to cover one month's rent. While I read and signed the one-page, handwritten lease agreement, she talked about various things, mentioning she'd been the choir director at St. Paul's and now taught singing to a few private students.

It had taken me a year to find a voice teacher in Kennebunk, and now I had met one here already. I was too shy to say I took lessons in Maine or that I liked to sing, but I planned to take lessons from her.

Returning on the plane, Roland read and I reflected on how alive I had felt in San Miguel. Like I did in Spain. And because I can speak Spanish, Roland made me his mouthpiece—he'd even asked me to do the talking with some English-speaking people—though I know it's not the same to talk if Roland asks me to rather than speak my own thoughts on my own initiative. I still find that hard, and know I have to work on it.

ଔ

Back in Kennebunk, I was faced with my second son preparing to leave home, to join Anthony and Antonio in Montreal. It was a major period for me, and though my emotions ran high, I didn't spend much time working through them or talking with Conrad about his new status.

At other times, I dismissed the matter by saying I don't have to provide a home now, his father could take charge. With no financial or other support from him, I'd raised Anthony and Conrad for thirteen years, and it was time for him to give support. I really doubted his ability to help financially or to give advice, and I felt some guilt at abandoning my parental role. The dilemmas I faced in my late teens when I had little money and no advice from my parents were so similar.

I stopped being closely involved with my children's lives at about the same time my parents had "quit" on me: when I was eighteen my parents wintered in Mexico, leaving me alone to decide what to do. Now I had plans of my own to winter in Mexico and for the rest of the year to work with Roland in a gallery.

After Conrad left for Montreal, I spent a couple of weeks in Kennebunk, fixing up our house for summer tenants while Roland worked in the gallery. One day he invited me for supper to see what he'd done.

At the entranceway to the living side of the loft, I wound my arm through his and we walked on unpainted, rough, pumpkin-pine in a living room so large it gave me a momentary feeling of weightlessness, where, if I had wings, I could take off and land. Roland's huge paintings covered some of the walls. A long and worn-out white couch, two matching chairs on shiny chrome rollers and a table was the only furniture.

The table was a piece of his art—he'd glued a four-by four-foot painting done on plywood onto a gallery pedestal turned sideways. The image on the top was of an abstract figure, like a snowman, outlined with black Conté crayon, and the whole piece was emblazoned with mixtures of rich deep reds, amber yellows and warm browns embedded in varnish. Roland's creative side had few boundaries...and I worried what was in store for me in that environment. *Will Roland find someone he likes better than me? Someone more like him?*

But he showed me around with such tenderness and pleasure that I derailed those thoughts. The fixtures and walls in the kitchen and bathroom came from a combination of his makeshift design and from a demolition site. Down a hallway beyond the bedroom, he'd installed a door that opened into the other side of the loft, the part that contained the gallery, my office, and his studio.

"Oh, Roland! What a place!" I said, "You've done so much." Shortly we ate his home-cooked roast chicken dinner, my favorite, on the coffee table. As it got late, the light from the one lamp magnified. I heard a pitter-patter scurrying motion, and looking down, saw several tiny mice darting in and out from under the white sofa. I pulled my feet up on the couch and could only semi-ignore the little creatures. I was going to sleep in their space, and begin to take it over, starting that night. I felt a little sorry for them and briefly thought of all the changes going on in the world constantly.

☙

In early July, shortly after I started spending time in Portland, Diane, my former H&R Block client, came trotting up to me on the sidewalk in front of Danforth Gallery. "Helen, how good to see you! What are you doing here?"

I pointed to our sign. "Roland started up a nonprofit gallery, and I'm managing it."

"I can't believe it—my studio's in the same building! What a coincidence. Do you want to have lunch together sometime?"

I'd never been invited to lunch before by someone I didn't know well, and the invitation surprised me. But I readily agreed. What a good way to get to know someone better—and maybe someday I might be brave enough to ask someone out for lunch myself.

I was especially surprised by Diane's expression of delight at seeing me, her income tax preparer! I didn't have a good opinion of tax preparers: I saw us as instruments of a necessary, unpleasant and boring chore that many people hated to do by themselves.

Diane visited our gallery a few days later, "Oh my gosh, Helen, I can't believe it! You and Roland—my income tax preparers—had this artistic creativity in you all along! I love Roland's art, and your living space is to die for."

After I explained to her how the gallery worked, she talked with Roland about joining the Advisory Board and I got to know her better that way. I liked every single person on the seven-member board and was getting to know many of them as individuals, on a personal basis, when we met to discuss certain particulars for an exhibition. It was the first time in my life when I dealt regularly with people whom I found likable and interesting. I had a few lunches with people, including with Diane. It was all new and exciting. I felt a little bit like floating on air and, although I never landed with a thump, I didn't make much progress in relationship skills because most of the topics I discussed with everyone remained exhibition related.

ᘓ

Our activities were largely tied to events at the gallery. Our monthly income from the sale of the income tax franchise barely covered our personal expenses–not enough to go out with our board members to plays, concerts or for dinners. Roland tried to make money from selling his paintings in other galleries. Although several gallery owners liked them, nothing sold.

For the most part, Roland stopped helping me with chores in Kennebunk now that he had Portland to look after. In August, I went to Crescent Surf more than he, but he joined me on weekends. When we had tenants, we stayed in the Old Garage, which we now called the Pool House, being that it was in front of the swimming pool.

I still loved Crescent Surf, although I saw no one in my family. I'd sit on my little upstairs balcony in the Pool House, trying to stay out of sight from the renters on the large deck next door. *What would Nana and Aunt Llewellyn think about my renting our house? About sleeping in a loft where mice ran around my feet? About all those ugly old appliances and furniture? About my dedicating myself to help artists? About Roland–my spouse who's discovered so much joy and energy from painting that sometimes I feel left behind, much like a little girl running to catch up with her family, crying out, "Wait, wait for me!"*

ʚ

With fall came the first function the Advisory Board organized. For nights, I'd lain awake imagining everything that could go wrong, wondering why I agreed to run a gallery. The course I took at Harvard on ancient and pre-Renaissance art was of no help. The only other knowledge I had about art came from the Sixties when I was in Spain and saw paintings by Velasquez, Goya and El Greco and, recently, what I saw in Mexico. Most of that art was by artists who were famous but dead, whereas the ones I'd be dealing with now were living and wanted to get known.

When the day came, three youthful pleasant-looking artist-photographers, out of breath from having lugged an odd-looking huge old table up the two flights of stairs, knocked on the door. Then they brought up bags of art supplies and a fresh, two-foot-long bluefish.

At ten o'clock, six people, dressed in the sort of clothes I wore when I painted around our house, showed up. They proceeded to draw the bluefish lying on the table in preparation for making silkscreen impressions of it. Around eleven they stopped drawing and turned toward some box-like structures with screens on one side.

I paced the floor in the living side of the loft, and occasionally walked by their table. I didn't try to understand the process. It didn't interest me, but then the instructors set up an electric frying pan they'd brought to make soup from the now cleaned and cut up fish with some vegetables. One artist asked me for a can opener, another for a big spoon. I watched them consuming soup and overheard them say that eating the fish made the experience more complete.

Around four I looked in while they were cleaning up. I turned away smiling. *Artists will be all right to work with. I may even like it.*

Confronting Shyness

11
Observing Others

I wanted to learn how to appreciate art, so I wouldn't feel so out of place at the gallery. Not wanting to reveal my lack of knowledge to anyone else, I turned to Roland for help. Visiting the Portland Museum of Art, I linked my arm in his as we looked at a Winslow Homer painting. "Okay, Roland, what do you like about this painting?"

"Each painting should have a focus–in this one it's the boat. The painting should make your eyes move all around."

"But, what if I don't like the work?" I asked.

"Some art's no good. Homer's is. Notice Homer's quality of drawing–that can add a lot to a painting. Some paintings have more drawing in them than others. Some have none. Today, drawing's becoming less important, and some art schools don't even teach it, but for me it's always been important and I consider the ability to draw essential, no matter what kind of art you do."

In the following months, after we left an exhibition he would ask, "What piece did you like best?" and we often agreed, which pleased me because it showed I had a discerning eye. After two to three years of viewing art, I had confidence to reveal to others which pieces I liked and why. Having this skill allowed me to feel more comfortable with artists and it helped shed my reticence.

One day I asked Roland what I was supposed to see in a painting he'd just finished.

"Let the art speak to you. Don't worry about what you think you should see. Just stand in front of it and don't think about anything. If parts of the work cause you to be drawn into it, that's good. It's an interactive process and very subjective. I know it may sound strange, but I leave a part of myself on each canvas and it can speak to you."

Leaving a part of himself in each painting sounded most interesting, but I didn't really understand it. I believed he meant he left a little of his soul there, but this outpouring of his internal thoughts was so unusual and welcome, I didn't want to ask what exactly he meant for fear of discouraging his openness. I was enjoying the mysteriousness of the art world; it made me feel as though I were involved in a transcendent process. I started to worry less about myself, to be less self-conscious, and that too eased my degree of shyness.

The Advisory Board's principle function was designing exhibitions with innovative, imaginative and exciting features to assist the artists advance their careers and to help the public understand and appreciate types of art that weren't usually shown because they had little commercial appeal. The board planned shows for novice and established artists, for local artists as well as for ones from other parts of the country. No art form was excluded and, if we didn't offer an opportunity in a certain area, anyone was free to present a proposal to the Advisory Board of his or her own design. That first fall in 1990, the board laid down the framework for six exhibitions for 1991.

It thrilled me to belong to such a creative group and, though it often seemed daunting, the challenges involved in doing so many tasks left little time for feelings of inadequacy. My job required that I talk with Advisory Board members both before and after board meetings, something which I especially enjoyed because it brought me closer to everyone. At meetings, I took minutes and asked ways to accomplish what needed to be done, such as who to ask to do the graphics and who or what business might give financial support for a particular show. I may have appeared calm, but inside I was as excited as a child learning to ride a bicycle.

My new cohorts were not just creative. They were kind, generous and supportive. After a dozen meetings, I felt comfortable enough to add suggestions, using my imagination, initiating a sea change in my self-expression. I didn't speak about personal thoughts there, of course, but offering my own ideas to enhance exhibitions made me feel more valuable.

I can see now that I spoke with ease in the group and with other artists because the gallery and my work provided structure for conversations. But there was little need or time for small talk, the casual kind of conversation about which I still had no notion. I wasn't making any friends, and at the end of the day I was alone with Roland, but I had less time to fret over it.

To be sure, many times I felt like an impostor, not knowing much about contemporary art or artists. In addition I had difficulty understanding our mission statement: the words didn't make all that much sense, kind of like I was unable to pull together a philosophy of my own because I didn't understand key value-related words even though I'd heard their definitions in my epiphany. From time to time, if I asked Roland, he'd explain it to me, but the gallery's mission still seemed vague and I was too shy to ask him to slow down and explain how the various concepts fused to realize our goals. In particular I didn't understand just how we benefited society and I was petrified someone would ask me. But in twelve years no one ever asked about anything except logistics, such as our hours or how to get his or her art shown. I guess everyone else in the art world understood what we were doing.

I only knew I was working with dedicated people at something more meaningful and rewarding than anything I'd ever done, so I went ahead more or less blindly, with enthusiasm. In a few years I was given the title "director" instead of "manager," which made me try to focus harder on what we were doing, but even so, it took me a couple more years to realize the full implications of the importance of our work for the community at large: we brought a variety of art to people and helped them to understand it, all for free. This seems so simple a concept for me to state and understand today. I believe that my mind was so embedded with personality-related issues back then that I didn't think clearly.

During the very first show I coordinated, called "The Essence of Maine," I learned some tremendously important lessons about people in the art world. For this show the Advisory Board suggested I ask Martin Dibner, perhaps the best-known art critic and enthusiast in all Maine, to be the juror.

After a worrisome night, I sat down at our makeshift table of plain unfinished plywood in an otherwise empty gallery and called him. I feared he might ask me something about art, for example, about something in a particular show. I wouldn't be able to answer anything about any exhibition, anywhere in the world, and this could cause him to resent the fact that such a novice sought him out.

But when I asked him to help, he replied with not the least hesitation, "I'd love to! When do you want me there?" I later learned he was volunteering his time, as would eventually multitudes of people who supported our cause simply because they loved art and organizations and directors that made exciting and purposeful exhibitions happen.

When Martin came to jury, I studied him in order to learn about the selection process. I started to observe differences that included technique and expression as well as matting and framing. And I looked for the qualities Roland taught me.

About twenty artists, their spouses, most of the Advisory Board and a few members of the public came to the opening of "The Essence of Maine." Unlike today, when many people wear ordinary clothing to openings, then everyone wore something special, like a batik scarf or a shirt made of rich colors, to signal they belonged to the art world. I walked among the crowd... *This is perfect. I never have to wonder what to say to anyone or stand on the sidelines feeling left out. People come up to me with questions and comments, and if no one's doing that and I feel left out, I can refill food plates or go to the kitchen for some quiet time.*

I can't believe how pretty the lemon yellow catalogue is. To think the government sent us the image of the state emblem to put on the cover! All the artists thanked the Advisory Board, but they especially clapped for me, for my effort.

People stayed for two hours eating everything the restaurants gave us, and some artists volunteered to transport and install the show in three other cities while we were in Mexico. Several newspapers wrote lengthy, illustrated articles, helping to create a name for the Danforth Gallery and excitement for the artists. One work sold: a tiny painting of a rowboat for fifty dollars, and the gallery received 10 percent commission. It was rare for us to sell anything. Beauty isn't an essential quality of alternative art, and homeowners more often than not wouldn't want to display the work we exhibited because it didn't evoke warm feelings or provide typical, pretty images that would make their homes feel cozy.

I observed something else in this first exhibition. Even with all the advertisements I gathered for the catalogue, after expenses there was no money left for me. I wondered why Roland, who did the accounting, didn't set aside at least something, if only a token, but I was too shy to speak up. I didn't want to disturb the wonderful gallery happenings by speaking about money for myself. Over time, it became apparent Roland planned to spend any surplus to make the gallery more attractive and expand its image. Ironically, he didn't know it couldn't continue indefinitely without paying someone to manage it.

With all my work I had little time for loneliness, but on Christmas Day I felt homesick and called Montreal to speak with my sons. Roland was cleaning up after our abbreviated turkey dinner, cooked in the loft with a two-burner stove and a small electric oven. Not much light came in through our one small window on that short, sunless day and, while I waited for someone to answer, the dark in the corners of the living room magnified. *Everything's different. Our house is closed down for the winter and my children aren't here. What kind of a family are we when we don't live together? What's ahead for me with my children? How do I get to be with them? I miss them so, but I don't see how it can be done and now it's time to head south.*

ᘓ

In January 1991, Roland and I fell in love with San Miguel again. Right away he asked me to line up exhibitions for him at the two principal galleries. I enjoyed preparing for those exhibitions for two reasons. I was very much in love with Roland and wanted to help him and, through being involved in his life, I acquired goals in the outside world, something I still couldn't establish on my own. The shows gave me many people to talk with, such as printers, gallery staff, framers and newspaper editors, and invariably I went back to each person more than once, for one reason or another. I enjoyed any opportunity where I could practice and improve the art of conversation; not being able to participate in small talk, I cherished having a purpose.

When I met with Mexicans, I conversed in Spanish, using their polite indigenous manners: not rushing, always saying "hello" and "goodbye" and, in addition to dealing with the matter at hand, allowing for conversation to develop about whatever either of us thought important.

Not understanding a word of Spanish, after such a discussion Roland often said, "What on earth were you talking about?" when it took me five minutes to buy something as simple as nails for concrete walls. Roland liked to stick to the matter at hand while in conversation, maybe in a New York fashion, but I sensed that Mexicans enjoyed exchanging ideas with me, maybe because few foreigners spoke Spanish. So I treasured these mini-dialogues of diplomacy and goodwill and kept right on having them. Besides, it felt so good to converse with people who overtly showed appreciation for me. I would have loved to have some Mexicans for friends, to learn more about their culture, understand their outlooks, but with Roland not speaking Spanish and my lack of social skills, we never made Mexican friends.

Even though I was busy helping Roland as well as overseeing household matters, I had plenty of time to be introspective. I observed people, including Roland, who seemed relaxed, who seemed to enjoy life and asked myself, why can't I relax? I knew I had to learn how before I could feel that I belonged to the universe the same way my epiphany said I did five years earlier. Over, over and over, I wrote in my journal I wish I could learn to relax—to have confidence in myself, to be more outgoing, to have friends. My confusion and unease is apparent in the following excerpt I wrote that winter:

> Goals, now I am starting to get ready to set goals, but this will by nature be difficult, and, of course, they may be changed. But one should never be without a goal! Short-range goals are to develop more self-confidence, not by doing and thinking, but by practicing. Have more of a social life with meaningful friends. Dress up more. Another goal is my reading program.

I finally embarked on a goal, music. I still ached when I heard certain beautiful music because it reminded me of never learning to play the piano as a child, being locked in my room, and in general of my unfulfilled relationship with my mother. I believed the only way to cure this was to become involved in music myself. (Later on I would examine my relationship with my mother while working with a therapist.) So, I got up courage to ask Jane, our landlady, if she would give me voice lessons.

She told me, "I don't teach very much, and I only do it because I like to, so I don't charge much—five dollars per lesson. I don't have a piano, just this little keyboard, and I lost my voice—I used to be able to sing five octaves. But, come once a week and I'll see what we can do."

We worked on half a dozen well-known Mexican and American songs and several scales, all of which I performed at the weekly lesson and daily at home. I was excited when Jane said my voice was beginning to develop, and especially later on when she said, "Why, Helen, you have a beautiful voice!" Rather than allow my feelings to shine through, I looked out the window so she wouldn't see my tears. How I'd wished I'd been able to learn music as a child!

Sometimes two musicians, acquaintances from the Unitarian group, invited Roland and me to parties. I stood mostly by myself, not knowing how to join in.

Gosh, I'm almost fifty and I'm still not me! I cover up my personality talking about things I'm not all that interested in because I don't know what else to say. Maybe people notice my lack of sincerity and leave me alone because of it. It drives me crazy to see all these people here talking, laughing and having a good time, especially since they're musicians and I love music but I have no way to share those feelings. It's like the pain from my childhood still dominates everything, keeping me mute.

Fortunately for me, my friend Nancy enjoyed the duties of the minister's wife (Royal was the non-paid leader of the Unitarian Universalist Fellowship in San Miguel). She asked me to be in the choir and I joined. From its vantage point, I scanned the attendees–about a hundred, largely retired, and mostly white people from the United States and Canada. Some lived year-round in SMA, but most were snowbirds, as we North American people were called, and some were temporary visitors. Few were Unitarians or Universalists back home: people attended services to socialize.

Having been an English and drama teacher, Nancy also directed short plays, usually written by U.U. authors, and we performed these during the regular service time. She must have known how much I needed opportunities for personal expression because she always saw that I participated. It seemed she didn't falter at much in her life, and a bit of her pluck rubbed off on me.

For the play *The Cloak* by a U.U. author, Clifford Box, she gave me the role of the unborn spirit. I can see now how that role suited me! I'll never forget her incessant coaching to teach me to enunciate my one big line: "I can see far away on the mountaintop, way beyond the steamy river and the dark green forest," in such a way to give life and meaning to the passage.

When the Sunday of the production arrived, I wore a long white sheet with a light blue sash. Instead of speaking fast and low so few would notice me, I deliberately drew attention to my words to create emphasis. Nancy's presence gave me courage to perform, and I found I loved experiencing expressivity in front of people. I felt as if I had passed a hurdle in overcoming shyness.

Around this time I attended a series of workshops on personality growth led by a Dr. White, a psychologist from the U.U. Fellowship. At that time, San Miguel was a mecca for people seeking self-discovery, and it was not unusual for visiting professionals to provide classes. Many, including these, were free.

Eight participants signed up and after we had spent an hour together, she asked us to voice our first impressions of one another. The time came to describe me. They all agreed I exuded a leave-me-alone, cold demeanor. And this when I wanted to make friends! It was like a disaster; I wanted to become invisible. But I was there and couldn't run or hide as my turtles used to do.

The therapy worked, though. Days after getting over the initial shock of hearing others describe me, I began to search hard for the basics for making conversation and friends–abilities I'd sought my whole life. I realized the formula for achieving rewarding discussions and for making friends lay in expressing WARMTH. I'd been taught in childhood that showing emotions revealed a lack of proper education, and as a consequence, I thought it undesirable to even have feelings. I had to unlearn that concept.

I understood that in order to make my epiphany come to fruition, I had to get to know myself and then like myself–two goals I'd known were important, but had simply just never paid much attention to. It was a variation of the golden rule–love yourself so you can love others. Dr. White's sessions helped me to accept myself as I was, including my shyness, and to be more patient with growth. Just knowing I was on a course for developing friendship helped soothe my feelings of social isolation.

ଓ

Conrad called me in Mexico. "Mom, I'm joining the Air Force!"

When I hung up, I was angry, not at him but my relatives. If they hadn't blocked my subdivision plans, my land would have sold by now and I could have provided a better education for Conrad. I vowed that if anything bad happened to him, I'd sell all my property and move far away.

Roland had his own viewpoint. "The military's the best possible place for him. If they can't do anything else right, they know how to get people to learn. And the Air Force treats their people well."

It was now April first, time to put away my notebooks on growth, pack my clothes and head back to Maine. Roland's exhibitions in San Miguel went well, and though he didn't sell much, several collectors said they liked his work.

ଓ

That spring in 1991, I practiced some of what I'd learned from Dr. White–showing warmth–during an exhibition called "MOMA," curated by my former income tax client and now Advisory Board member, Diane. In this show, artists showed renditions of mothers, some with children, using clay or wood sculpture, paintings and installations. How could I pretend to like this show when it reminded me of my unfulfilling relationship with my mother and made me feel wretched? But, being the gallery manager, I had to hide my feelings and show enthusiasm!

One installation was a large image of a mother with a child sculpted in wood. Draped in a light blue shawl, she was frowning while looking at her baby, who had hardly any facial features. Curious, I looked at everything in the show more carefully, and found a painting of a girl staring strangely at her mother. Although I didn't care much for any of the art in "MOMA," I was happy that two artists shared unpleasant experiences with their mothers, like me.

I concentrated on these two artworks, and afterward, talking with the artists and viewers, expressed warmth and genuine admiration for the exhibition without saying what I liked about it or why. To do so would have required me to talk about my mother and my childhood, and that would have been too painful. I learned an important lesson: when I was being genuine, expressing warmth came quite naturally and made me feel more connected to others. I started to smile more. I'd always considered myself sincere, but lacked the wherewithal to reveal it. By now too, I was learning that artists tended to be genuine and this helped me to relax and relate with them.

Many times I wished Kathleen would visit the gallery, to see what I was doing, but she never did, and I considered it an imposition to ask her. We rarely saw each other and I missed her. When I called her to do something together, she always responded positively, but she never called me and I felt something was wrong, though I didn't know what. Now I think she might have considered it unprofessional to call a former patient.

ℭℜ

I phoned Anthony about his upcoming graduation. "Oh, don't worry about coming, Mom–it's not important." I recalled the bitter disappointment at my own graduation when it seemed everyone but me had family present. "But, I want to come, Anthony!"

It was one of the few times I spoke up and acted! I felt liberated. I was defying my parents by breaking family tradition and attending my child's graduation. I knew I was doing the right thing, but also that I was poorly equipped; our land still wasn't selling and I didn't have a nickel to spare for the trip.

But then, using some of our scant resources from the sale of H&R Block, I bought a pair of brown Rockport wingtips for Roland; he wore them subsequently when dressing up for at least ten years, always referring to them as his "graduation shoes." I also got him a black wool jacket onto which I sewed gold colored buttons we'd purchased years earlier in New York, with the emblem of his alma mater. And I packed a pretty pink suit Roland had given me for Valentine's Day.

We drove, and about halfway there, Roland said, "Oops, I think I forgot my jacket!" Then, driving in downtown Montreal, the hood of our old Jetta blew open into what seemed like our faces. We struggled to find a mechanic who worked Saturdays to fix it. We did, and the next day I felt proud as only a parent could, watching my son graduate in the magnificent, large pink and gold-colored theater at McGill. Why hadn't my parents wanted to see me graduate?

The following day the university held a casual, outdoor get-together. We stood near Anthony and his roommate, an honor student in engineering from Mexico, and his parents. The graduates sashayed around saying goodbyes and several came by to see the roommate. Not one came to see Anthony. I wondered to myself if this was the reason Anthony had not shown much interest in our attending: he didn't want me to see he had no friends other than his roommate. I was saddened; Roland didn't seem to notice. The curse of shyness stabbed me over and over. Then all of a sudden, I noticed Anthony seemed to be bearing up all right. Staring at him, his eyes appeared to speak, "Hey, Mom, it's all right, I'm doing fine."

Roland and I drove back to Maine and Anthony followed a couple of days later. In my fantasy world I still thought he was pretty sophisticated and would achieve an important career either teaching or doing research at a university. Soon enough I understood he had other aspirations. I asked as casually as I could, not wanting to sound probing, "What would you like to do now that you're out of school?"

Sitting on the floor in his bedroom, with a big map on his lap, he looked up and said, "I want to take two to three years and hitchhike around the world, doing odd jobs along the way."

Nothing could have shocked me more. I remembered what had happened to me by living in so many places—I never got around to developing a career and now I feared Anthony could miss out as I had. Right after that thought, I panicked over another idea. With his slight build and quiet temperament, I envisioned thugs stealing his knapsacks and bicycle and leaving him in a pool of blood on some back road in a country where he didn't speak a word of the native language.

He went on to display self-confidence of the sort he hadn't shown since Outward Bound, several years earlier. "I don't see any point in the way people live around here." Moving closer against the wall, he went on, "They're not interested in anything but going to some job they really can't stand and buying what they think they must just to keep up with their friends."

In many ways I agreed with him about the boring work and social frenzy. Today, I realize how fortunate he was to have had a world outlook of his own at such an early age. At the time, I only tried to convince him to think twice about the dangers in traveling the world alone with no money. After a few months, without explaining what had changed his mind, he went to live on a cattle and coffee ranch that the father of his friend from McGill owned in southern Mexico.

☙

I met Jane and her significant other, John, when they attended the opening of one of our shows, and this gave me something to talk about with them when we met again at an artist's party. Roland and John began outlining an art project and Roland invited them both to our loft for further discussions and lunch. It was about the only time Roland ever initiated a social event.

On the day of the visit, with a bright smile, and a heartfelt "How nice to see you," Jane entered the loft and changed my life. Feeling her warmth, I responded with a big smile of my own. Roland took John aside to talk about his work.

Being an accomplished interior decorator and owner of a historic fabric store in Exeter, New Hampshire, my guest knew how to dress. The rich brown of her slacks on her trim figure set off the pale turquoise in her knitted sweater; her delicate purse and the silk scarf around her neck suggested a sophistication that I liked but lacked in my own attire.

Jane had large, clear blue eyes that dominated a face covered with freckles. She pinned her wavy auburn hair back from her face with pretty clips. She spoke in a soft, warm voice, listened attentively and smiled with enthusiasm when appropriate.

I usually felt awkward standing up and trying to make conversation with someone I didn't know well, so by habit I asked her to sit down. Shortly, she jumped up saying she wanted to see Roland's art—the dozens of four- by six-inch paintings he'd spread out on one section of the pumpkin pine floor. I stood around for a few minutes with everyone and then went to the kitchen.

I fumed a little as I poked the potatoes. It seemed as if Jane were more interested in seeing Roland's art than in getting to know me. But when I brought the food to the table, the atmosphere improved. Jane raved over the salmon, salad, peas and potatoes and was impressed I could prepare everything with a two-burner stove. Everyone but me had wine, because I still wasn't drinking alcohol, and the meal turned into a delightful occasion as we discussed our varied international travels and, especially, our mutual fondness for Mexico.

John and Roland returned to the art, and, still sitting, Jane turned to me. "I look forward to the four of us getting together, and I hope just you and I can have lunch sometime and go for a swim."

I didn't need to think before I replied "I'd love to." We set a date for the following week. When they left, my heart raced, and I asked myself over and over, could Jane become a friend? She acted like one and talked like one!

The following week, with a little trepidation, I joined her on the white sandy beach in Ogunquit—a town halfway between her house and mine. She led the conversation. "When I was a child, I used to come here with my father. When the tide was going out, we'd float down the river on our backs."

I listened closely, and trying hard to be genuine instead of letting worry over my shyness affect my conversation, said, "I used to swim in Kennebunk, on our family beach. An uncle used to throw me into the waves when I was only three, and I always asked for more."

Then we talked about each other's deceased great-aunt—hers was as instrumental in her life as Aunt Llewellyn had been in mine—and from there it was but a short step to discussing the most important part of our lives, our men. I was being open, free and loving it. We made plans to swim again soon.

Before Roland and I left for San Miguel, John and Jane agreed to visit us there the following year; meanwhile Jane and I would write over the winter.

Yes, I had found a friend. It felt wonderful.

12
Participating More

During the winter of 1992 in San Miguel Allende, in addition to arranging more exhibitions for Roland, I concentrated on self-expression, mostly at the Unitarian Fellowship. I was turning fifty and though I didn't feel at all old, I realized my life was more than half over and I was still very shy, and worse, so very full of hurt.

I decided to tackle the matter face on by singing in public. My landlady and now singing teacher Jane had said I had a beautiful voice. So, though I'd never sung alone in front of anyone other than her, I set out to do a song at the Unitarian Fellowship, to celebrate the start of the second fifty years of my life with an act of bravery.

Nancy, who knew me well, and knew I wasn't a soloist, never questioned my decision. She said, "Talk with Royal and get a date." I spoke to Royal right away and he asked me what I wanted to sing. "It's a pretty piece by Foster called, 'Was My Brother in the Battle,' about a woman who lost her brother in the Civil War."

"Oh, good," he said, looking pleased, "sing it on Lincoln's Birthday when I give a talk about him and the Civil

War." Now that I had committed myself, I practiced everyday at home for a month, listening to the song on a cassette and using the bel canto technique to the extent I knew how. I was too shy, however, to tell my voice teacher what I was doing and get help from her.

When Lincoln's Birthday Sunday came, when the pianist played my song, I was forced to perform. I stood behind the audience, beside the piano in the back of the room, so I didn't have to look at anyone's face. But as soon as I opened my mouth, fabrics rustled as everyone turned around to see who was singing. I told myself to concentrate on the song and to fill my voice with strength, beauty, and feeling for the woman who'd lost her brother.

Afterward, the pianist said I did all right, much better than in the two rehearsals–which she'd given me somewhat reluctantly because she thought I didn't sing well. And not without justification, for, when rehearsing, I'd felt too shy to lift my voice with any expression. I was elated it had gone so well, but most important, that I'd fulfilled my vow and knew I could set more difficult goals in the future.

Roland said little. But how could he or anyone be expected to understand my degree of torment connected to music? How would he know it symbolized being shut in my room and failing to learn to play the piano? Or know the ripping pain I'd internalized since childhood because I couldn't express myself in any fashion? On the other hand, Nancy did seem to know, without my telling her about it. Unfortunately, she couldn't be present–she'd been diagnosed with cancer and was home in pain.

We left for Maine in time to attend the Danforth Gallery's first major exhibition of 1992, "A Visual Ode to the Book."

For this exhibition Jeffrey Haste, a printer and an Advisory Board member who often helped me by designing brochures and invitations, selected thirty accomplished Maine artist book-makers. The books were made from all kinds of materials such as iron, handmade paper and wood, and assembled in a variety of sizes, shapes and colors—and this work astonished me.

Every day (when no one else was there—which was usual) I touched and examined the art, pondering the time and thought that went into making it. One book in particular, the size of Webster's Unabridged Dictionary, stirred my curiosity. Made from heavy, dark metal, the artist presented it on a brown wooden base that resembled an old trunk, making the book appear as solemn as a body in a casket.

It was my first time to experience the art in our gallery as being something more powerful and paramount than myself. By deflecting attention from my shortcomings, it gave me a new freedom, inviting me to explore the unknown, allowing my ideas to search for their own creation. This transformed into encouraging me to take more concrete steps to understand myself.

☙

Although everyone on our Advisory Board was highly creative, I loved Roland's ideas more than anyone else's, and I learned how to do things mainly from him. I saw him sit for hours at his desk and witnessed the struggles he took to assemble carefully thought-out, effective plans. Some of his ideas came from examining art organizations' bulletins and arts magazines. But he also went beyond the journals, deriving some of his best ideas from his lively imagination. His creativity became apparent to viewers in the ways he presented our exhibitions.

For it wasn't enough for Roland to exhibit interesting works of art. He also wanted to give a unified concept so that viewers observed the pieces as part of a meaningful whole. The Director of Contemporary Art at the Maine Arts Commission, Kathy Ann Jones, told us Roland was the only person she knew in Maine who could do that.

That summer I became quite aware of this gift of Roland's in an exhibition Diane designed for us, called "Children Portray Adults: Adults Portray Children." For this show, I solicited hundreds of drawings from third-grade pupils and their art teachers in the Portland area.

Roland appeared when I was covering the gallery walls with the art for it. "That's a lot of art. Let's try to break it down..." he mused, ambling around. "Let's build a wall covered with some of the art, starting by the door, and"—moving about ten feet out from the entrance—"have it come out to here, so when people come in they feel like they're going almost through a tunnel, into something special. It'll create a passage into the child-adult place." I was amazed at the difference the change made.

I realized that creativity, that intangible quality I'd first encountered in English 101 when reading Chaucer's *Canterbury Tales*, was the artist's principle tool. My life centered around artists now, and I began to want to learn as much as I could about being creative when the opportunities arose.

However, Roland did so much for me I didn't need to be very creative. As he did during the years we worked at H&R Block, he gave shape and direction not just to our work, but also to my life. Self-pity and a lack of self-confidence, leftovers from my bleak childhood and adolescence, still limited my ability to initiate things on my own. Sometimes, when I decided to stop feeling sorry for myself I went to the beach, splashed into the cold ocean, focused on the gallery and on what I had to do next. For the most part, I allowed the gallery's exciting goals to become synonymous with my own.

Sometimes when Roland saw me awkwardly trying to talk with people, later he'd give me ideas when we were alone, such as "Set out tools people need to hang a show before they come so they don't have to imposition themselves by asking for them" "Don't feel you have to explain yourself. People accept what you do" "Before you speak with someone, try to see where they're at mentally, so you don't interrupt their chain of thought" "When you ask someone how to solve something, don't offer your ideas, just tell them the situation, and ask them what they think. People come up with better ideas then" and finally, "Don't apologize that you haven't done certain things; it's unnecessary. People accept situations as they are."

I appreciated his giving me these suggestions–but much more important, because of them, I noticed I got along with people better!

Consequently, my spirits were good when we flew to Mexico. I was looking forward to seeing Anthony who had tired of the ranch in southern Mexico and was going to live with us in SMA for the winter.

ଔ

Eight years had passed since my epiphany in 1985 urged me to be receptive to and believe in universal love, and yet I still had no world outlook of my own. For the most part, words like *compassion, fairness* and *trustworthiness* remained vague concepts: I did not feel the inherent importance of these values, nor did I consciously practice them. Now, not having a philosophy of life bothered me as much as it did when I'd attended the University of New Brunswick.

As a consequence, to learn about it, I decided to give a talk at the Fellowship called, "How People Develop Their Sense of Values," and for material source, I interviewed a couple dozen Unitarians. Normally, I was not brave enough to initiate a conversation with people I didn't know well, so I doubly enjoyed the discussions: I was getting to know and talk with people and also learning about building value systems! I spent over an hour with each interviewee asking a list of written questions including these: "When were you first aware of such a thing as a sense of values?" "Did your parents discuss values with you?" and "When you became older, did you adjust your values?"

People seemed to like the process and often delved into their childhood with nostalgia. I'll never forget one woman from Montreal talking about learning the value of sharing as a little girl while she walked in the London subway. "Mom," she asked, "what good does it do to give that poor man a couple of pennies?" "Well, if several people give him a few, he'll have enough to buy something." I wondered why I hadn't asked questions like that when I was little; her question sounded profound to me. Another interviewee told me that all people were born with the devil in control of their souls, and that parents and teachers had to constantly try to enforce goodness. In addition to learning about values, I learned people are different and complicated.

When I gave the talk, everyone sat quietly, and I wasn't sure if that meant they were interested in the topic or if they were waiting to hear how I would present what they'd told me. I enjoyed that morning because I felt close to a few of those present whom I'd interviewed and afterward, a few people told me they found my talk interesting.

Meanwhile, of course, I didn't breathe a word to anyone about my personal confusion over values. I thought they might consider me audacious to give a talk on something I knew so little about, but the experience helped me conceptualize philosophical values. In fact, the process no longer seemed so mysterious because now I understood that having a philosophy consisted in how I saw the world and my relationship to it and about what or who was important, worthwhile, or loving in it. I knew my ideas would expand, but for now, I was relieved that this talk constituted a sound beginning for my world outlook.

In addition to self-expression, I received another lift from participating at the U.U. In a structured group conversation that I myself organized and led, I was able to talk and thereby assure myself I had a probing mind and interesting ideas, even if shyness continued to restrain me from expressing thoughts at parties and in other casual settings with peers.

☙

Roland and I arrived back in Crescent Surf with more optimism than usual because a sale of some of our land was imminent: money was scarce. The Department of Fish and

Wildlife had tried to buy some of our land for decades in order to expand their property at the adjacent Rachel Carson Wildlife Refuge. We'd given them the go-ahead and they were preparing the paperwork.

At the gallery, I was impatient to earn a salary, but I just barely managed to raise enough money from the arts community, granting organizations and businesses to cover the overhead. I brought it up to Roland, who said, "It's not just you; I don't get anything. Nobody gets anything. We have to pay the expenses first. You know that." "But our costs keep growing; I'll never get anything." "Well, we can't help that. Work on selling the land. That's a certain income."

Roland's attitude bothered me. It ignored my efforts in the gallery and the reality that the gallery owed me something. I swallowed my hurt, though, because I didn't have the courage to stand on my own.

I liked the work of gallery director, but beyond that, Roland and Portland offered me little. When I stopped work for the day, boredom set in while Roland kept busy painting and reading. Our poor financial situation meant we couldn't go out and have dinner with people or go to the many cultural activities happening around us. We stayed in the loft's living space until bedtime with nothing but the television and one or two dim lights. Sometimes I got angry with Roland about our lack of money, making the evening worse, although it broke my habit of silently caving in to him. The fact that I could start an argument with him somehow bolstered my self-respect: I was standing up for myself and expressing my disappointment.

I now had three homes to manage in Maine: the main house, the Pool House, and the loft. Between them and running the gallery, I was too tired to dwell for long on money problems, but I also still felt emotional pain from Roland's lack of warmth, my up-and-down parenting and the scant contact with my relatives.

Finally, the sale with Fish and Wildlife materialized, and they became the owners of most of the sixteen-acre subdivision. Half of the proceeds went to my brother, and with mine, I paid off my share of the mortgage on the house and a couple of smaller loans. I set aside money to buy the house in San Miguel, which had gone on the market. I felt relieved to know I wouldn't have to worry as much about money and that none of the sales would anger the relatives—they were delighted to have the land used for conservation. And Nat and I still owned plenty of land.

☙

During the ten years I lived on Prince Edward Island and would visit my grandmother in Maine, relatives apparently believing that Canadians spoke French as well as English, would ask if I spoke French. That surprised me because I'd never heard anyone speak it, although we studied French in school. Now, I encountered a similar situation. Although clusters of French descendents lived within ten miles of me in an old mill town, I didn't see many signs of their culture. I decided to curate an exhibition by artists of Franco-American descent. With that in mind, one beautiful Sunday afternoon in August, Roland and I caught the tail end of a statewide conference on Franco Culture. The conference leaders embraced our ideas with enthusiasm, and immediately assigned individuals to assist us in any way we needed.

They provided us with a graphic designer for the show and he came up with the title "Migrant Within" because, he explained, "We Franco Americans are always unhappy with where we are and we move around a lot. We're so confused we don't even know what to call ourselves." When I didn't ask, he offered, "The most accepted way seems to be Franco Americans."

After several months of acquiring art from around the state, I organized a gala opening. Several restaurants, including a specialty delicatessen in far away Lewiston, donated generous amounts of tourtière, a traditional French-Canadian pie made with potatoes and ground pork and some good red wine to accompany it. We hired two Franco-American musicians to play the accordion, fiddle, and to sing and clog dance. Having anticipated a large attendance, we opened the living side of the loft for the food, beverages and entertainment, keeping the gallery side to view the art.

At my request months earlier, Roland had painted the floor in the living portion a cheery light green because on Prince Edward Island we once had a painted green floor in our kitchen, and I'd liked it. Now, conversations, music and heartfelt enthusiasm expressed by a hundred and twenty-five Francophiles all colorfully dressed and moseying around on the green floor created a spell of magic. Being able to utilize former experiences from my life on Prince Edward Island in order to make so many people happy made me feel accomplished and purposeful.

To provide more depth to the exhibition, the Advisory Board suggested we have panel discussions by Franco Americans about their culture. I assembled five prominent professionals from different universities around Maine. In the discussions, they recounted how their families had rejected their cultural inheritance because they felt it was inferior. For example, as children, some parents had told them not to reveal their family background in school by speaking French, so they sat in silence as much as possible until they learned English. We, the audience, felt their bitterness and sadness.

I felt a warm kinship with them because we both had histories of isolation. I sensed that as I undertook an active role to help them to expel their feelings of inferiority I was in effect helping to overcome my own.

Roland and I transported "Migrant Within" in our new, blue-green Taurus station wagon to five distant towns in Maine and New Hampshire. At each place the panelists assembled and we videotaped their discussions. Five of the biggest state newspapers wrote full-page glowing reviews.

Sometimes I was so excited about this show I couldn't sleep, but at the same time I had concerns. *How can I work so hard with so many talented and important people, have our shows get rave reviews, yet not be able to raise much money? It's exciting and I love it but it's degrading that Danforth Gallery doesn't receive more financial support. Roland's no help.* I didn't have a background in art so no gallery would hire me. I think that not receiving an income ultimately helped me, gave me a little push to stand on my own two feet and to discover what I really wanted to do with my life.

ଓ

Roland and I went to a concert given by the Sea Glass Chorale at the oft-photographed South Congregational Church in Kennebunkport, the one I attended with my grandmother. When the friendly and vivacious director announced she welcomed new singers and she didn't require an audition, I made arrangements to attend the next rehearsal. About seventy-five people from the Kennebunk area and I rehearsed weekly. We prepared Christmas songs for two churches and *The Messiah,* at a third. I felt good belonging to a large singing group and had little difficulty following the music for the soprano part.

Some people appeared quite social during breaks while others kept to themselves. I remained aware that it wasn't easy for me to initiate conversations. Sitting alone during one break, I wondered why singing didn't make me all that happy. *At our openings, I see the exhibiting artists' beaming with joy. I don't feel that about singing. I think the artists feel something very special because they feel passion for their work. I want to feel that. I don't have a passion. Singing isn't it. What's wrong? Why can't I find my passion?* But I continued singing because I enjoyed doing it more than anything else.

13

More, So Much More to Do

We stayed in Maine that winter until the opening, on February 14, 1994, of a show called "My Funny Valentine," which Roland helped curate. At Roland's urging, we went by car back to Mexico, taking six days, going through places whose names I couldn't always spell.

When we arrived in SMA, Anthony was preparing to go to Venezuela, where his father now lived. I was happy for him because he was looking forward to working as an adventure tour guide near Angel Falls.

In March, Roland suggested I volunteer to review the SMA International Film Festival for the local English language newspaper, *La Atencion*, and the editor approved. I cannot remember the names of the films, but I enjoyed the whole process: watching the films, summarizing them and, especially, expressing my viewpoints. Many were in Spanish with English subtitles and my two favorites were Mexican. One illuminated intriguing and shady maneuvers in an intricate web of law enforcement in a rural area a couple hundred miles north of SMA and the other showed lives of criminals, prostitutes and drug addicts in the suburbs of Guadalajara under the dark of night. I felt professional and intelligent to be able to use my mind to cover such exciting artistic endeavors. At the end of the film festival, during the gala party, although we didn't speak much with anyone, I didn't feel as uneasy as I usually did at gatherings because I felt I belonged there.

We had a major exhibition coming up at Danforth Gallery in April and when the time came to return to Maine, we were eager to leave.

ꝏ

The buzz began well before the opening: Paul Caponigro, renowned as one of America's most significant master photographers, especially of nature, was showing at our gallery. It marked the first time in about twenty years that Caponigro, whose home was in Maine, had shown on the East Coast. Everyone connected with the gallery helped, and by this time there were plenty: the Advisory Board, a few interns and about fifty volunteers.

On the day before the opening, I answered a faint knock on the living side of the loft and saw a dark-haired man of about my height with an enormous radiance. When he spoke, his voice was deep, beautiful and firm, resonating so gently it sounded more like a prayer. When he moved across the room to meet Roland, he made few movements, almost as if an internal engine glided him. For me he was likable in every way. Not being a talker, in addition I was now too in awe to say anything, but I smiled a lot, and he responded in kind.

The first thing he did was to acknowledge the catalogue of his photographs that Jeffery Haste had made. "I always hesitate when people do a catalogue, but this is really a fine job!" I especially liked it because Jeff gave me credit for my work at the gallery on the inside cover, just above the Library of Congress serial number.

During the opening for "The Voice of the Print," large numbers of people from Boston to Bangor politely sidled up to speak with the charismatic photographer and as many returned two weeks later to hear him talk about his work. That time everyone sat on the floor with their heads turned expectantly, as Paul, perched on a table, gave them stories about shoots in many parts of the world. The gallery had been transformed into a receptacle for expressions of beauty and wisdom.

There was one photo that sparked particular interest and I noticed some people going "ohhhh," after studying it. So I looked long at it and after a while the twisted trunk of an old tree in a wheat field morphed into the shape of a sexy woman. I felt creative to be able to see the image.

☙

At our request, the University of Southern Maine and Maine College of Art referred students to us to do internships. One of the requirements for the interns was to spend a certain amount of time on particular projects, so I got to know several of them quite well. I compared what they were doing to what I did in my early twenties and admired their confidence. It was rewarding to help them and be a part of their growth, for, although I'd missed out on the growing part in my youth, I sort of experienced it with them as I watched their self-confidence blossom with the successful completion of their assignments.

Some interns were painfully shy. They liked working with me, and a couple stayed for two and three years. Others were outgoing and sailed right along in their programs, eager to leave and go on to their next activity. It was interesting to observe both types.

By 1994 shyness and its consequences no longer bothered me much at the gallery because I was so busy. But, as soon as I left our four walls to attend an opening in some other gallery or museum, I felt inconsequential, lost and just wanted to go home.

☙

That winter at the Unitarian Fellowship in San Miguel I met Greta, fifteen years senior to me. Her outgoing friendliness drew me to her. She had taught yoga for many years, and convinced me to attend a slow movement yoga class with her. I attended for two months and was learning how to relax my mind and body. Then the instructor Katrina took me aside one day after class. "I noticed you don't have much male energy. By doing this simple exercise, called Fire of Breath, you can develop some. Watch me, and do this twenty or thirty times first thing in the morning."

She raised her arms straight up and held them rigidly. Then she jerked them downward, straight out in front of her and did a simultaneous up-down snapping motion with her eyes without moving her head.

After a few weeks, my whole body energy changed—I felt considerably more emboldened. Well, maybe I wasn't all that bold, but I felt a little braver and loved it. I did the exercise for several months until my mind somehow permanently stepped up its flow of "male energy," and I felt mentally strong without doing the exercise. Thank you, Katrina!

I had always been a person of little physical stamina compared with what I saw in others. I figured I was just made that way, and nothing could be done about it. Also, I had low blood pressure and thought maybe this accounted for my lack of endurance. My mother recommended I lie down and rest before special events to conserve my energy—a habit I continued.

The same winter I met Greta and Katrina, I learned some powerful dynamics of physical energy quite by accident. SMA is 6,500 feet above sea level, and while walking up the hill to our home, often I had to sit to catch my breath. One time I sat down and found I wasn't out of breath.

What's happening? I've walked this hill three days in a row and I'm not out of breath. I feel fine. This is incredible. Can it be that the more effort I put out, the more I have within? Having more energy is the key to everything. Imagine resting up all those times in my childhood before an event—now I suspect it just made me weaker. I wonder, is there a snowball effect in everything people do, from physical exercise to showing warmth—the more warmth you give out, the more you will have within? The kinder you are to others, the kinder you will want to be?

ര

For me, Roland captured a special feeling in his art like no one else. I found his work intriguing, inviting, colorful and, best of all, simple and intricate at the same time. I loved his art like I loved him, and I wanted to be with both, forever, even though living with Roland could be demanding and difficult. He left me alone while he worked and didn't talk much when he wasn't working. He seldom spoke about our relationship, my wish to have an income or about my need to have more friends. When I pressed these issues we wound up arguing.

I knew his rationale by heart. "I do my painting, and you look after your own needs. I need to do what I'm doing. All I can do is paint and use the little time I have left to concentrate on my work. It's what I have to do. Every great artist has a big ego–it's what propels them onward, to work day after day, turning a blank piece of paper into something, with only faith that it will become a work of art."

In late March, Roland had a show called "No Hay Agua" at the Museo Allende. He was happy when someone stole a small piece. Meanwhile my friend Jane and I corresponded about our artists' egos–about the burden we accepted in order to enjoy the better parts of our men.

In the middle of April, we flew to Boston and had to go by van to Portland because heavy sleet grounded the planes. I cringed as we drove through Kennebunk. We dashed right by Kennebunk, my home, as though it didn't even exist. Roland probably didn't even think of it, and for me it was so important.

ᘓ

By now we were doing twelve provocative and exciting exhibitions a year. Artists, viewers and reviewers raved about Danforth Gallery so much our phone constantly rang, people knocked on the door and my "to-do" list grew ruthlessly.

Our busiest period to date was September and October of 1996 when we opened four major exhibitions. For September, Brad McCullum, a new member of our Advisory Board and a Yale graduate, curated "Exquisite Corps: A Sculptural Installation." The idea came from an old French parlor game where one person draws part of a human body on a piece of paper, folds it over and passes it on to three more people and the four segments form a human shape.

From four accomplished university art instructors in Maine we received the following: for the head, large sculptured shapes of male and female genitals covered with chocolate syrup; for the shoulders, dozens of opened jars of milk that soured long before the three-week show ended; for the body, a mass of metal bars and, for the legs, several boxes of moss complete with instructions to spray daily with water.

Every other day I skirted the smelly milk to spray water on the moss and thought, *I don't get this. What's it about; why'd they do this? The artists are well known but they didn't give us much to think about. Even Roland hasn't commented on it.* The show stayed up for most of September and barely a dozen people came to see it.

Then in October we opened three shows at three different venues. Rosalind Purcell, a nationally known museum curator and published author from Boston, selected photographs for "Visions of the Mind: on the darker side," an exhibition of work from all over the nation. In the prospectus,

Rosalind called for photos that "elicited universal responses of foreboding, apprehension or fear."

I secretly wondered what kind of a response we would have; would it be a flop? Would people reveal their darkest thoughts? Wasn't I one of a few with gloomy sides to me? My fears didn't materialize: hundreds of photographers submitted slides, and Rosalind selected about forty-five "eerily depressing" ones. The work fascinated me, and I started to realize the extent to which dark ideas existed in people. It made me feel much less alone with my old pain and the shame that went with it.

For another show, based on a model we'd seen in Mexico, Roland curated "The Forest City Annual: 1996 Wood Sculpture Exhibition and Symposium," a site-specific, national wood sculpture show. (Portland is known as the Forest City.)

Fifteen artists from around the country came to town to build or erect their work on Main Street. One artist from Boston designed five seven-foot-high grandfather clocks from plywood and placed images and artifacts of old Portland where the face of the clock would normally be.

The night before the opening for this show, I boiled a lobster dinner for the artists. Too tired to sleep, I tossed in bed until about midnight. The next morning I looked terrible and could barely keep my eyes open, but we had three nationally known art writers convening for the opening symposium. We didn't have much seating capacity at Danforth Gallery, and the Portland Museum of Art allowed us to hold the symposium in their large auditorium. The museum director, not Roland, announced the program, and, while she mentioned us, I didn't feel that most people in the crowded auditorium would understand that Danforth Gallery had been responsible for organizing everything.

But I derived an important lesson from this exhibition. The volunteer graphic designer, the head of the Maine College of Art Graphic Design Department, created a most extraordinarily magnificent poster, invitations and even some very special stationery for it. Through seeing these talented people help us in order to help the community, I realized I'd been blind not to see how valuable our work is. I've been focusing on myself, on my lack of credentials, on my lack of professional knowledge. We were putting on outstanding shows and now I could see how unique and important we were. When I tried to raise money from businesses, I understood I might do much better if I expressed and emphasized these community benefits.

Three days after the wood sculpture opening, another show, an annual one by artists over fifty-five that I curated, opened in a restaurant in Ogunquit. It required extra planning because it traveled to several towns. With so much happening I didn't realize my mental energy was depleting, but shortly after the last opening, I was drained. I couldn't even remember some of the things I needed to do, and eventually, I realized I was suffering from fatigue and burnout. I had dozens of volunteers, but it tired me just to provide them with tasks, be supportive of their efforts and supervise their work.

I tried to take it easy and told Roland the gallery was becoming too much for me. He replied, "Be patient. Just keep trying, and we'll eventually be able to pay you."

"But can't you see, even with pay, it's too much work for me?"

"We'll hire someone to help you, too. Besides, we can't close now. We have too much going on here."

How on earth would we find money to pay for two people when we couldn't for one? But with Roland arguing got me nowhere.

☙

Anthony had sent several faxes describing his employer and his job, leading tourists through the Venezuelan jungle. He'd wanted Roland and me to visit for a long time, but I'd been too busy with the gallery. Now I was so happy to be doing something special for him, to show I loved him, and also pleased I'd been able to give him some money from our land sale to help him start a business of his own.

Roland was eager to go as well because he wanted to paint at the University of Merida, in the small city of the same name in the Andes where we planned to stay a month. We left on my fifty-fifth birthday, December 3, and over the Caribbean, Roland surprised me with a beautiful sparkling red gem called a spinel, on a slender gold chain.

At midnight, in warm drenching rain, Anthony met us in his Toyota jeep at the Caracas airport where he too gave me a present and a bear hug. After a day's drive across the plains, the winding road narrowed as it ascended the Andes. The next day we stopped for the best breakfast of my life: freshly made arepas, a national dish made from white ground corn topped with creamy butter, homemade blackberry jam, and coffee, made from beans like those we'd just seen drying beside the road.

Merida lay in a long, narrow bright green valley between two snowy mountain ranges. Anthony's Venezuelan friend told him it's called "the honeymoon city" because it's so pretty, and the climate is ideal year-round. In a couple of days, as soon as we found an apartment, we drove to the University Art Gallery. As in Mexico, I did all the talking. I asked the young female attendant if Roland could paint in a studio for a month. She directed us to the head of the Arts and Science Department, who ushered us right in to see him. He didn't know of a painting space for Roland, but after finding out where we were from and what we were doing in Merida, he was kind enough to send us to the director of Cultural Affairs for the entire county, to see if he could help. In turn another cultured, polite and soft-spoken man gave us names and phone numbers of the best artists and museum directors in the region.

To meet with the people we'd been referred to, Anthony took us to museums, restaurants, art openings and to several private homes and studios in Merida's mountainous artists' colony. Almost everyone invited us to eat or have a drink with them after showing us their studios, homes and art. No one spoke English. I did all the talking, loving it. Anthony was often ahead of us somewhere, talking with some younger person or on his cell phone. The artists were impressed by the video of Roland's art, but since he spoke no Spanish, they spoke to me about everything.

It felt so good to be talking with so many well-educated people, who seemed the friendliest people in the world. They appreciated our company, we eventually learned, because most Venezuelans at that time had little money and almost no contact with the outside art world. We had a gallery and knowledge of the art world they craved. (Through our assistance, one professor came to Maine that summer to give a workshop.)

But not one person answered my question about a studio space for Roland, and after two weeks, bored with not having a more active part in the social activities, Roland grew impatient. "Helen, for heaven's sake, call Alfredo"—the first person who helped us at the university—"and ask him point blank: 'Will Roland have a space to paint or not, and if so, exactly when and what will it be like?'"

I hated to put anyone on the spot, especially these helpful people, and Roland's questions sounded confrontational. Yet, it was as if Alfredo was waiting for my call and knew that Roland wouldn't be happy with the truth. "During the Christmas holidays the private university painting studios are closed. Roland could use the communal studio, but no, he couldn't have his own key, and no, there is no place where he could lock up his materials. No, there are no windows, just electric light." Roland threw up his hands when I relayed this: "All this for nothing!"

Anthony left to go to Caracas to pick up his tourists for a three-week trip the day before New Year's Eve. I hadn't tasted a sip of alcohol since July 1985. Now I decided to drink again: to have one or two drinks at a time and never when in an agitated or depressed mood. So we sipped champagne and listened to the first of some fireworks that went on all night. It felt good to drink with my new healthy accord with alcohol.

In spite of Roland's disappointment, for me the trip was sensational. I basked in the afterglow of having talked and expressed myself so many times with such carefree and pleasant people. Glancing down at the green Panamanian landscape on the return flight I relaxed, thinking about how wonderful it was to see so much of Anthony, day after day, in the environment he'd chosen to live. Even Conrad flew in from the Air Force base in Biloxi, Mississippi to join us at Christmas. I loved the wool sweaters and funny hats we bought for the trip up the 15,500 feet to snowcapped mountains in the cable car. Then for six hours we rode mules down the other side, down a rocky path so close to a precipice that Roland turned ash white. Being by ourselves in the rustic hotel–even the owners were away–in the tiny medieval farm village Los Nevados was special. Years had passed since we four had been together.

☙

In the Venezuelan art world, my shyness retreated as much as it did when I visited Italy, more than thirty years ago. When I arrived in Mexico, although it didn't surge up as suddenly as it did when I arrived back in New York after the trip to Italy, it did return slowly. The pain from my youth, the hurt buried deep inside, was still capable of holding me hostage.

☙

I always tried to present Roland's work in the best format I could, with the politest personal manner possible, and I knew from being a gallery director what that meant: having an easy-to-read résumé, a few samples of invitations and catalogues assembled in an attractive portfolio, as well as talking with the director, not in a pushy fashion, but rather allowing him or her ample time to think, ask questions and visualize how the art would fit in with the rest of the gallery's shows.

The director of the Diego Rivera Museum, known as El Maestro, also held the title of Head of Cultural Affairs for the State of Guanajuato. He agreed over the phone to look at Roland's work, and I took charge of preparing the materials for the interview. Roland and I fought for days over what to select from his impressive, ten-page curriculum vitae for a mere two-page résumé, one I insisted on, suitable for the interview. The arguments got so bad, we discussed divorce.

I finally assembled what I thought was pertinent and found a printer who did a splendid job using gold highlights. He prepared a glossy white folder with Roland's painting name, Salazar, written in his own handwriting, in the same gold color, on the cover.

Roland tended to talk too much at interviews, not allowing the director time to think, so I asked him not to say much. But since El Maestro spoke only Spanish, with a beautiful voice, it was not an issue.

I plunged right in. "We just want to show you Roland's résumé and a few small works he did this winter, from a series of twenty four- by six-inch diptychs."

Roland handed the printed materials and paintings to El Maestro and sat back. Glancing and nodding at the glossy white and gold folder and its contents, El Maestro examined each piece of art. His face became as serious and solemn as an Olmec statue. The pieces in his hands were among my favorites. Done on heavy, durable paper with rough edges, each of the twenty gods had a corresponding landscape. Immortal-looking faces astonished the viewer with direct gazes and expressions that reflected an acceptance of their fate. The colorful landscapes invited not just the gods but also the viewers to hide amid canyons, to walk among rolling hills or to sit beside a cactus plant. Roland's love of distortion characterized each piece in free and loose drawings.

After what seemed a long, long time, El Maestro looked up. "You know, in all likelihood, we'll have a cancellation in December. The exhibition would last for two months. Could you show then?" We assured him Roland could. He walked us through the museum, pointing out the four rooms he would have, three of average size and one extra large. We knew that showing in this museum was an honor reserved for only a few artists. The visiting artist shared the museum with only one other, the great Diego Rivera. It was April, but Roland started planning right away.

We flew back to Maine with our hearts full of anticipation. The purple lilac trees planted by Colonel Hart in the eighteenth century never seemed to have bloomed with such rich intensity.

ଓ

Roland's art is so good. But how do I fit in? I have nothing to show, not even a personality that feels good. I just have to do something to feel better about myself.

I knew full well that in order to feel better about myself, even though it would be excruciatingly hard, I had to deal with the pain from my childhood. I chose my first good friend, Jane, with whom to broach the topic.

Selecting the right moment, as we sat in front of the water in Ogunquit, our feet warmed by the sand, I lowered my eyes and, with caution, turned my head partially away from her before I spoke.

"When I was a child in Connecticut, I was locked up in my bedroom." My eyes dampened and my throat constricted. I could say no more. Jane didn't push me to continue, instead said that it hadn't been uncommon in the past for parents to do such things in New England. I felt sure most children probably hadn't been locked up as frequently as I had, but I didn't want to say any more about it.

I changed the topic. But I'd broken down the door to the wound, and that felt magnificently weird. I knew now somehow or other I was going to be free, freed of the past. I would collect my thoughts about other aspects of my childhood to tell Jane on another occasion. I was determined to share my stories with her, and with others.

Conquering Shyness

14
Confidence and the Mind

In late fall of 1997 I felt better about my family and myself. Anthony was leading tourists on adventure trips in Venezuela and Conrad was working in Boston, using satellite maintenance skills he'd learned in the National Guard. Roland was preparing for the show at the Diego Rivera Museum, and, on this splendid day, I was meeting with Diane, my former income tax client and now a treasured acquaintance on our Advisory Board, at the Wordsworth Bookstore in Harvard Square to search for books for my development.

For the first time, I wanted to look into shyness as it had been examined by others, and bolstered by Diane's presence, purchased three books on the subject. I felt like an explorer, as if I were embarking on a complicated journey to the core of my being and I worried over what I would find. However, after we left the store and said our goodbyes, I tucked the books under my arm with a new feeling, a good one, one of self-respect.

ଓ

We left for San Miguel earlier than usual that year, the second of November, because Roland wanted plenty of time to prepare for his show at the Diego Rivera Museum. Needing to take several materials from Maine for it, he loaded our station wagon with his supplies until we could just barely see out the back.

At the annual International Jazz Festival in San Miguel, I noticed the editor of *La Atencion*, Sareda, sitting right behind me. I decided to ask her to review Roland's exhibition.

About five-ten in height with a thin build, she had close-cropped brown hair that nicely framed the angles in her makeup-free narrow face. I'd seen Sareda perform lead roles in plays and musical productions around town since my first year in SMA and had often asked myself how a person could be so involved, so outgoing. I was very unlike her.

I had had almost no contact with her other than the half-dozen times when I submitted articles for the Film Festival and other events I'd covered for the newspaper. She'd dealt with me in a friendly and business-like manner. In a curious way, she knocked at my inner door, as if asking to see if my personality would come out and play.

Taking a deep breath, I turned around. "Hello, Sareda. Roland has a show coming up at the Diego Rivera Museum in Guanajuato in December. Do you think you could review it?"

"By all means, call me when the time comes."

☙

"Helen, you're late! Get moving! Call the framer and see if he has my pieces ready yet."

I disliked Roland commanding me to do things in that way, but by now I expected him to be unpleasant before an opening, and this time we were both unusually excited and on edge. Roland had almost a hundred paintings ready for his showing at the prestigious Mexican museum. He'd named the exhibit, "With Your Permission, Gods, Land and People of Mexico."

Dozens of people came to the opening, most of whom, speaking no English, congratulated Roland in Spanish. El Maestro stayed by his side, introducing him to guests. I was so proud of him. All evening I glided around observing, smiling and enjoying myself, wearing the woven silk shawl Roland had just given me, a silver one with beautiful, long, white embroidery. It matched my frilly black skirt.

At the end of the evening we walked up some stairs in the four-story building to get some things we'd left in the upper office. He stopped midway and glared at me. I saw his face was contorted and his eyes had become dark pits. "You think you're a goddamn queen." I gave him a look of exasperation, said nothing and continued ahead of him. Why did he say that? What was wrong with him? I knew asking him would only make it worse.

His insult wounded me. Not only was it unfair (why shouldn't I take delight in his success? I'd struggled with him and supported him all these years), but something worse bothered me. It had been a rare occasion for me. I was looking pretty and feeling happy, two things that alleviated my weak self-image, and he'd ruined it.

Roland's never going to help me feel good about myself, ever. He only thinks of himself. I'd just love to leave him right this very moment, but where would I go? My life's so mixed up in his...the gallery, our house, his exhibitions. I don't know what I'd do on my own. It's so infuriating.

I simmered for a few days. Maybe he'd had a miserable time at the opening because he didn't understand the language. He may have wanted me at his side to interpret, but I hadn't thought of doing that, not wanting to interfere in his moment of glory. Besides, he always could have asked me to join him. But I didn't think of any of this at the time of the remark, and by then it was too late to do anything about it anyway.

Swallowing my hurt, my life with Roland returned to normal. I called Sareda, and about a month later, a full-page glowing review with three images in color appeared in the bilingual Mexico City newspaper, *El Universal.*

ය

To nurture my self-confidence, I chose to give another talk at the Unitarian Fellowship. I'd often thought about the haphazard quality of my spiritual growth and decided this would be the topic. I would call it "Unitarianism from the Heart," because all my information for the talk would come from within. I set a date in early March to allow two months for preparation, enough to give it plenty of thought. I worked hard, rising before dawn on several occasions. Ideas came to me most clearly at that quiet time, when my mind was fresh and the neighborhood asleep and, if I was lucky, ideas from my sleep world would materialize to broaden or deepen my perspective.

I organized the entire service and presided over the selection of three hymns, including "Not in Vain the Distance Beacons," which I dedicated to the memory of Nancy Cloyd, who loved its beautiful words and powerful music by Beethoven. I longed to do the Unitarian version of "Onward Christian Soldiers" in "silent" memory of my grandmother who'd taught me the original words when I was growing up in Cos Cob, but I feared I'd cry. For the closing reading, I chose "The Heart Knoweth" by Emerson, the soulful mystic as enthralled with nature as I'd been on Prince Edward Island.

For twenty-four hours before the talk, I did nothing but preparation, eating lightly, exercising and focusing on the task ahead. Reading my paper aloud, I made little indicators on the pages to tell me which words to emphasize, where to pause or look up, and where to raise or lower my voice.

The Sunday came. I was cocooned in concentration. Standing in front of the hundred and twenty people sitting on green plastic chairs, I kept in physical contact with the hand-crafted wood podium. By being a physical constant every Sunday, the stand symbolized for me other people's searches for growth and it gave me assurance that I had the right to talk about mine, too. In addition to the eighty year-round and winter regulars, my audience consisted of short-term visitors from all over North America who wanted to attend a Sunday service in English. To my right stood our Fellowship's pride and joy, a Dusseldorf grand piano whose sound touched the souls of even the tone deaf.

I began with the beliefs I held about God during my years on Prince Edward Island, especially what I learned at

Sunday School and the ideas I developed when I rode my horse over fields and through the woods during all kinds of weather. I described the absence of religious thought during my adolescence and I spoke about my father, whom I credited for many of my Unitarian beliefs.

Throughout, I directed every ounce of my strength to following my paper and remaining calm. I knew from a drama class I'd taken for my teaching degree in Calgary to look at an area in the back of the room, a little above the audience's heads, so I wouldn't see anyone at all. But after I read, "I went from the Greenwich Country Day School to a two-room schoolhouse on Prince Edward Island," a woman sitting in the fifth row in front of me gasped. For a split second I went faint, wondering why. I thought maybe she suspected how disastrous it must have been to go from a prestigious school to a two-room one, and how distraught my mind must be now, which I had not intended to imply. But I managed to return my focus to my paper in a seamless manner and continued. I ended by saying where my heart's journey had taken me:

> My heart says, be sincere and avoid arrogance, envy, and trivial matters.
>
> My heart says, be moderate, but have the courage to speak up so that those who tend to be loud aren't heard everywhere.
>
> My heart says, be kind and pay attention for signs of kindness in others.
>
> My heart says, cherish soul-mates because the spark that kindles these friendships is the spark of the universe, and it is this spark that will make my life shine for myself and for others.

I hadn't thought about what would take place, if anything, when I finished the service. Approximately a third of the people rushed up to me. I could barely make the transition from my presentation to conversing with people. Some said how much they liked what I had to say and how hard it must have been to write it. Others just touched me, but all of their responses were warm.

I was exhausted but still running high on adrenaline, and I looked around the room at the others to see their reactions. I saw some stand up quietly, shaking wrinkles from their clothes or straightening neckties. I wondered if they were thinking, "Well, that was a waste of time." Roland, who preferred talks about empirical theory to material from the heart, shook my hand thoughtfully, saying, "It went well."

I didn't care about the rest of the audience who seemed indifferent. It absolutely delighted me that so many expressed unabashed enthusiasm.

I just spoke from my heart. It must be that not many people do it. I wonder why not...are they afraid? Embarrassed? I'm so very pleased to be able to say what's really meaningful for me—all my life I've been hiding my thoughts. But something must be keeping other people from being forthcoming...I wonder what it is. I'll keep my eyes open to see if I can learn what.

As I walked home after the service in a warm glow from the appreciation people gave me, I wondered what else was important in my life that could serve as a topic for another talk. I decided that whatever it would be it had to come from the heart. Unbeknownst to me then, the idea of writing about my troubled childhood was incubated that day.

ᘓ

When Roland and I left Venezuela a year earlier, Anthony gave me a well-worn paperback written in Spanish, and finally I read it. Called *Doña Barbara* by Romulos Gallegos, it's the most famous novel ever written by a Venezuelan. Constantly using my dictionary, I studied intricacies of the Spanish language, and in so doing noticed subtleties in human behavior. The author memorialized the sense of lawlessness common in some parts of the country, especially in the south where few people lived, where independent-minded ranchers changed boundary lines and rustled each other's cattle. The disorder in their lives made mine appear innocuous, and I relaxed a bit more.

Many times I'd felt slighted because of some comment I deemed rude, when in reality, the person who made it hadn't meant to hurt me but instead was misbehaving because of a problem of his own. While reading this book, it comforted me to learn many people experienced being offended in this way, and we all have to deal with it.

I'm so naïve to be learning this in my fifties. Will I ever be at peace? How long is it going to take!

Next I leafed through two of the three books on shyness I'd bought in Harvard Square, and was disappointed–they focused on how to find a mate! I wanted to get to the roots of this wretched curse, to eradicate it, to rid myself of it entirely, not to learn how to say something to a member of the opposite sex. Discouraged, I left the third one untouched.

But then I read a book Kathleen had recommended a couple of years earlier called *Flow,* by Mihaly Csiksentmihalyi. It contained prescriptions for a healthy mind, including how to develop self-confidence, lose self-consciousness, understand others, and control consciousness. I gave these ideas a lot of consideration and looked at my problems a little more objectively, easing some of their harmful effects. And in addition to ridding myself of harmful ways, the author provided me with concrete new approaches to look at the world; for example, in controlling my consciousness I learned I could think as I chose. I didn't have to be let down or hurt by others if I elected not to.

Then it was spring and I prepared myself for the drive back to Maine. It was my fourth continental road trip, and by now I knew I'd be sitting in the passenger seat for six days, semi-hypnotized by moving traffic, rolling countryside, look-alike motel rooms and French fries.

☙

Anthony called from Venezuela, which he rarely did because it was so expensive. I grabbed a chair. "Are you all right?" "Mom, I'm in perfect condition, so don't worry, but I'm quite shook up! The small plane I was on with twelve passengers crash-landed in the jungle. We're so lucky to be alive.

"You wouldn't believe what happened. To save time, the pilots decided to wait until Caracas to buy fuel. We left and when we were in the air and over the jungle the engines sputtered and stopped. We were so lucky. A pilot on a plane passing nearby answered our call for help and said he'd just seen a little clearing not far from us, and we managed to land in it. Two women were crying. It was awful."

"Oh, how terrible!"

"There's a bright spot, though. One of the tourists on the plane is a film star from London, Brian Blessed. Have you heard of him?" I had not. "He's climbed and filmed the Himalayas and played a small role in ***Star Wars***. He's quite a character, and he's writing a book called ***Quest for the Lost World***. He's going to dedicate it to me because he thought I did a good job handling the tour."

"I look forward to reading it, of course. Why did the pilots need to save time?"

"Ah! We were in Canaima, a little town accessible only by small boat, and they have to ship the petrol in. So they store it in large containers, and to fill up the plane they use little buckets! They fill one up, then scramble up a ladder to the top of the wing and pour it in using a funnel. It takes forever, and our pilots had to get to the Caracas landing field before dark because the plane has no lights."

Inside, I worried. I hated to have Anthony working in a jungle with people who take chances. I suspected he didn't tell me half of what happens. But he was doing what he wants. I was happy for him, I just didn't want anything to happen to him.

In August, Conrad called on a merry note. "Mom, can I bring Ellen around? I'd like you to meet her." I wondered if he was seeking our approval, or if he'd already made up his mind; I couldn't tell. Nevertheless, I liked the idea that he wanted us to meet someone special.

We gathered around the dining room table, in the upstairs living room of the Pool House. Ellen was pretty and calm. Her dark brown hair and even darker eyes contrasted with Conrad's light hair and blue eyes. While we ate she was quiet and unassuming, yet when she described her work—testing food appeal for military personnel in combat—she did it with warmth and enthusiasm. Conrad's eyes never left her.

Roland and I looked at each other with more than a little astonishment. What a wonderful daughter-in-law she'd make! I wanted to make my feelings known. Before she left that day, and in order not to embarrass Conrad, I surreptitiously gave her a small green silk scarf from Mexico.

Later I walked the beach by myself, impatient for my heartbeat to slow down. ***I'm so happy—I showed my feelings! It wasn't so hard, either. And I did it on a timely basis too. I feel so good—I'm making progress.***

In October, Conrad and Ellen told us they were engaged. Roland dashed out for champagne. I was happy to be able to give them a little financial help.

ꟻ

As we prepared to head south again, I kept thinking about how the mind functioned, and that maybe artists could help me find out. To this end, just before we flew to Mexico, I decided to curate an exhibition called "Danforth Shows the Mind." I spoke with an English professor and an arts instructor from the University of Southern Maine; the former gave me the name of a poet to contact in Mexico City, and the latter referred me to a current article about the mind in *Newsweek* magazine.

Roland commented little about my idea except to say it didn't have much focus on visual components, but I went ahead with my planning because the idea excited me so much.

Back in San Miguel I called Sareda who now owned a newspaper called *El Independiente* (in spite of the name, it was largely in English) to see if I could barter work for the use of a computer to communicate with volunteers at Danforth Gallery.

"Sure. I have a laptop I don't use. You can take it home and use it as long as you like. For the paper you can come in and proofread every other week."

To proofread, I sat in her one extra chair, a horribly uncomfortable one, almost behind hers, so it was easy to observe her while she worked. She kept very still while writing, but when she stopped to talk on the phone or attend to a visitor, her personality morphed into colorful conversation and soulful laughter. When she had no audience and wanted to talk, she spoke with her two gray kittens that slept on the warm air vents of her computer.

"Oh, yes, you little bugger," she cried out, "you're trying to keep your little sister away so I'll pay more attention to you, aren't you? Weeee, up you go! EEEEEH! Your claws are sharp! AHHHH, STAPPPPPP, STAAAAPPP!"

I likened Sareda's born-free disposition to riding on a zooming speedboat, emotions slashed loose, crashing through waves on an Amazon tributary. She understood my reserve, and I never felt uncomfortable with her straightforwardness. On the contrary, I felt protected around her in an unfamiliar way. She looked after weak beings, be they stray dogs, helpless kittens, or shy acquaintances. It surprised me that being protected was such a rare phenomenon for me, and I guessed it was because I hadn't received much of that kind of care as a child.

൏

In my study, the third bedroom called the Green Room, I looked through my books for clues on growing. I realized I still hadn't read the third book I'd bought on shyness, the one by Philip Zimbardo, a Yale graduate and Professor of Psychology at Stanford University.

Right away I saw this one was different. It wasn't about dating. Zimbardo accurately and sensitively described the fear and the hurt and all the situations I'd endured my entire life! He didn't offer quick and easy solutions, rather he gave plenty of helpful ideas and exercises to relieve the condition over time, to cure shyness from the inside out, for life. I read it slowly and carefully, underlining parts to go back to.

Zimbardo began his book *Shyness* by describing his mother's concern for his younger four-year-old brother, George, who suffered from acute social anxiety. She took him to kindergarten six months ahead of time to help him get adjusted, but he cried and cried, not letting go of her dress.

She came up with the idea of giving him a mask so he would feel no one could see him. The teacher went along with the idea, and told the other children he was wearing a special mask and not to remove it. George himself designed and made the masks from brown paper bags.

He wore one until the end of the following year at kindergarten. Then the teacher offered him the job of being the circus leader at the year-end party, but told him the leader had to wear a special costume that didn't include a mask.

George was so excited, and he did a wonderful job as circus master. Afterward he stopped needing a mask. Seeing his brother go to school with a paper bag on his head for eighteen months made an indelible impression on Zimbardo.

After studying this book, I suspected Zimbardo inherited his magnificent understanding of human nature from his mother. He made me feel he understood me and that I wasn't so strange after all.

I felt different, maybe a little giddy. *Gosh, I've been so in the dark! I'm so excited. I can't wait to be cured; now I know it's going to happen. When I was at the bridge club last week, I looked Ruff right in the face and held his gaze while I kidded him about a play he'd made. It felt so good.*

ଓ

I contacted Ms. Black, a poet in Mexico City, whose first name I forget, to get ideas for my show about the mind. "I'd be delighted to meet with you, Helen. I'll be in San Miguel the first week of February for Poetry Week. Come see me at my hotel."

The Sierra Nevada Hotel was the best hotel in town and I wondered what I should wear. Even though I was bringing a topic to our meeting and shouldn't have to worry about casual conversation, trepidation about talking with a poet kept me awake during much of the night.

Tall, slender, and dressed like someone I might see in New England, Ms. Black rushed right up to me because I was the only person seated in the hotel lobby. Her gray hair hung from her temples amid large, narrow-framed glasses that she wore partially down her nose. With a friendly but firm "How do you do," she sat down beside me.

"How good to meet you, Helen. Your exhibition idea is a challenge! I've given it some thought. Perhaps you can divide the show into five segments, each representing one of the five senses. For the visual one, the Spanish painter Remedios Varo would be excellent with her surrealistic symbolism. She spent many years in Mexico City."

After discussing some more details, I walked downtown humming, gliding over the old, narrow sidewalks made from square slabs of marble that ranged in hues from faded lavenders to dirty pinks.

What a kind and creative consultant this woman had been. I should try to be more helpful! I've always spent most of my time helping myself, worrying about me. I don't think about helping others. I hardly ever think about being kind! I want to work on being a more giving person. I bet it won't come too easy. But, boy it was fun talking with her. At last, at very very last, I had a conversation with someone without feeling uncomfortable inside. I could focus on the moment. What an accomplishment! I wonder if I can do it again.

I went home and drew floor plans of our gallery into five distinct areas, one for each sense, and thought about the brain. *Isn't there some other part of the mind that helps us think, rather than all coming from the five senses? Certainly all of our information has to pass through one of the senses to get to the brain, but the brain must have a special section just for thinking on its own. Good question to investigate, and I must know the answer before my show opens.*

I wrote a draft description for the exhibition, and afterward called Pam, a psychologist, and Dick, a wordsmith, who wintered in San Miguel and whom Roland and I met while standing in line at the bus station a year earlier. I told Pam about my idea for a show and she invited me right over.

While they gave me coffee, cookies and ideas about the mind, I observed the thoughtfulness behind their personal style, presentation and organization. When I was leaving, they said to come back–they wanted to go over my revised material. I realized how kind and supportive they were, as Ms. Black had been.

Later I became angry when Roland insisted that "Danforth Shows the Mind" wouldn't be a suitable show. "I'm not going to allow you to do it, Helen. I told you a while back that it doesn't have enough visual emphasis to it. Forget it. Leave it. We're not doing it."

I spoke back, "However lacking in visual abstracts, this volunteer director of ten years ought to be able to have a say in this."

"No, I'm not caving into your wishes; I'm the president, and I have to do what I think is right."

I stormed off, disappointed by his judgment.

Two weeks before Roland and I returned to Maine, Sareda asked me if I'd like to do the arts review for her biweekly newspaper. Inside I did a flying somersault. *I've never done anything like that. I cannot possibly do it. What on earth makes her think I can?*

"I can't," I said softly. "I'm leaving for Maine quite shortly. Thanks for asking, though."

As I packed, I felt dejected. *Why wasn't I more positive about writing the arts column? I could have said I'll do it next year. It seems Sareda has more confidence in my abilities than I do.*

15
My Big Discovery

On one of his adventure tours, Anthony fell in love with a British Hindu woman, Joy, and after five months of being in love under the same roof, they became engaged. I was happy he now lived in London, away from dangerous traveling in Venezuela, but I wished they'd chosen the United States, to be closer to me. However, they were coming to Crescent Surf for Conrad's wedding.

For the event, Roland painted the Pool House kitchen my favorite shade of yellow and I hung off-white brocaded cotton curtains made by a store in Oaxaca that my friend Jane recommended. My friends Carol and John, whom I'd known since university, stayed with us and helped with preparations.

I was happy to be preparing for a ceremony. A cycle of life! Now we were doing it according to tradition, unlike the weddings my brother Nat and I arranged for ourselves. In my only wedding photo, I wear a weary expression. It's Madrid, 1967, and I haven't one friend or relative present. Antonio has a friend—a musician—and several staff from the Venezuelan Consul were witnesses and attended the reception. A good party was had, but I only wished it to end because I didn't know anyone except my husband.

For Conrad's wedding, although my brother declined—I suspect from a form of shyness of his own—almost all forty of the Crescent Surf relatives accepted their invitations. The bride planned a catered reception for a hundred and ten guests in a white tent with a dancing floor on the front lawn, overlooking the marsh and ocean. About twelve of our friends were coming and Jane helped me select the perfect outfit.

After a beautiful ceremony at picturesque St. Anne's Chapel-by-the-Ocean in Kennebunkport, on the drive home I suffered from a nagging fear of being with so many relatives. I hadn't had much contact with them for over fifteen years, and now my emotions were spinning and churning.

Maybe I looked pale or just plain lost, but a few minutes into the reception, Jane grabbed my hand, said, "Come," and led me toward the house.

Inside she began, "It's customary to remove your hat once the reception begins. Don't you have a sweater or something to put on to change your appearance a little? Now is the time to relax; the big ceremony's over. Go out and say 'Hello how're ya doing' with people. Relax and have fun. You're the proud mother and a hostess."

I pulled out my silver shawl, slung it over one shoulder, took off my hat and lifted my face, and Jane said, "Perfect." I knew I could drink a few glasses of wine as long as I drank the equivalent amount of water more or less simultaneously. I talked with the guests and the evening became splendid.

In bed, just before I fell asleep, I sighed with relief. *I'm so blessed to have friends. And Anthony has a gorgeous fiancée, with round, luminous eyes as big as a horse's, and the kind of figure people used to worship for fertility. She's well educated, knowledgeable and has a great profession designing software programs, yet now they're off to Venezuela to set up their own adventure tourism business. I wonder if they'll be married here, too. That would be lovely. Another wedding. Big contrast between the jungle and London.*

Anthony and Joy left two days after the wedding. At first it was hard for me to think of my sons as being spouses, but soon it came naturally to remember their female counterparts in connection with them. It was good to see them changing, maturing. Anthony had taken everyone by surprise at Conrad's wedding when, in a rich, firmly metered voice, he gave a two-minute brotherly speech without once looking at notes.

☙

With my friend Diane at the Harvard Square bookstore again, I searched for material to study in Mexico. I asked the clerk what they had about extroverts and introverts and he couldn't find anything specifically about that topic, even with a computer search, so I bought *Personality Type: An Owner's Manual* by Barbara Thomson because it contained two chapters on the subject. Today there are a number of books about those two traits. On a bit of a whim, I also bought *Power Performance for Singers: Transcending the Barriers* by Emmons and Thomas.

Somehow I knew my self-growth depended on my own initiative. It was difficult because it was still quite new for me to do things for myself. Roland claimed he couldn't get involved in my development because he didn't know how to be of help. I wondered as we walked from the taxi into the airport on the way to Mexico why my husband, so capable in many areas, couldn't assist me. But a light snowfall caressed our heads and I stopped thinking about it.

ඥ

When I arrived in San Miguel in 2000, I rethought my ability to write the arts column. Roland and I still didn't have a laptop, so I would have to ask Sareda if we could borrow hers again. I was used to forcing myself to do things for the gallery that I wouldn't normally do for myself because of shyness. And if it hadn't been for the computer need, I might have been too timid to contact her and face the prospect of doing the arts column. I recalled her outgoing personality and how much I wanted to be just a little like her, and that I might start by being more daring.

I called her and asked if we could borrow her laptop again... "And, I'd like to do the arts column if you still need someone."

"Good! When can you come by? I'll have the computer with me, and I'll tell you how to get started with the column. You can write about any aspect of the arts you want in one thousand words or so. Have pictures and send everything to me three days before we go to press."

With my newspaper role, I could interview most any interesting, creative person I chose. Sareda had just about given me free reign. I myself compiled the questions, allowing me to ask about things I normally wouldn't dare to. For topics I included architecture, art on the Internet, exhibitions and what it was like for me to be married to an artist.

For the article on architecture, I arranged to see six homes whose occupants included the very architects who'd designed them. They enjoyed showing me around. One house, formerly an old warehouse, intrigued me in particular. Upon entering, the visitor saw an elevated square pool of water in the center of a spacious but otherwise empty courtyard covered by a translucent ceiling three stories above. The home replicated the traditional Mexican one with rooms leading off a central courtyard, but this place had three tiers of rooms and a glass ceiling.

At the rear of the first floor, a bright, spacious kitchen looked as if it were an art installation in an otherwise sterile gray-brown space. Shiny, dark-toned appliances and a multitude of brightly colored pots and pans hung near a big wooden table. On one wall, dried foods and spices filled several shelves in distinctive canisters.

After my article appeared, an architect I knew from the Unitarian group, one unrelated to any of the six buildings, surprised me with his assessment. "Good article. You can tell you know a lot about architecture." Deciding not to comment on my dearth of knowledge about it, I nodded, said thank you and changed the subject. But I felt so good: I'd met six interesting architects and wrote an article convincing enough to deceive a seventh.

For months Sareda said nothing about my writing, and, dying to know what she thought, I finally brought it up. "What do you think of my articles?"

"Oh, I like them, but then, I only hear from the public when they don't like something."

I was disappointed in this answer, but that afternoon she emailed me a more in-depth response. "Your writing shows intelligence, warmth and understanding, an unusual combination, and it comes across."

Because most artists like to be written up in the newspaper for the publicity, all those I asked agreed to meet with me, allowing me to talk with many interesting people I would normally never have dared approach. It was a challenging and interesting process, every minute of which during both the interviewing and the writing, I felt creative and purposeful, and as my self-confidence increased, my shyness lessened.

ଊ

For the first time in over twenty years, I played social bridge because I feared if anything happened to Roland—he was sixteen years older than I—or if I became restricted physically, then I would want to play. Also, I knew some of the conventions of the game had changed, and I wanted to become familiar with the new rules while my mind functioned well. I played at people's homes, but I really wanted to play at the Duplicate Club, where they played better and used more conventions, but I wasn't brave enough to just walk in alone without a partner.

Then an acquaintance from one of the social games, a Diamond Duplicate Master, gave me an invitation. "You're such a good player. You should be playing at the Duplicate Bridge Club. Come with me."

I had twenty years of competitive bridge energy welled up, and after we scored almost top in the first twenty hands, she said, "Slow down!" That burst my bridge bubble and our results became more average, but even so, we scored unusually high. My friend said I was a natural. Later in the evening, I felt calm, relaxed and fresh.

A few days later I realized that listening attentively to classical music created a similar process in my mind and produced similar results. With these two pastimes, I become so focused I'm unaware of people, time and place. I lose self-consciousness, which in turn creates a calming and rejuvenating effect. So that year, 2000, I learned that bridge and my favorite classical music help my well-being.

One of my new books, *Power Performance for Singers*, helps prepare singers using a training method paralleling one psychologists use to train athletes. The authors insist that any person with a minimally trained, good voice can sing well on stage if he or she follows their procedures. It seemed plausible. When my small singing group prepared to do a free concert at the historic Teatro Angela Peralta, I overrode my queasiness and dared ask a fellow soprano, "Want to do a duet?" "Oh, yes. I'll ask Jorge to play the piano for us. What do you want to sing?"

I selected "Noche de Ronda" by Augustine Lara; most Mexicans love his work, and we were singing to a Mexican audience in Spanish. To practice, I listened to the song sung in Spanish by Lara on a CD dozens of times at home, since Jorge, a busy medical doctor, could only rehearse twice.

For three weeks before the concert, I followed many suggestions from *Performance for Singers*. In one exercise, I focused on everything in the room for a few minutes; then on a tiny segment of something near me, like a spot on my hand,

and then I switched back and forth. In another I imagined a special place where I did nothing but relax. I selected a sun-warmed sandy island in the South Pacific with one palm tree and just enough room for one person, me, to lie underneath. The goal was to go to the island at will, when I wanted to be calm. I also repeated a variety of exercises to deal with unexpected noise and disruption, ate recommended foods and established a sound sleeping routine.

I followed the advice about singing, too, such as memorizing every single syllable, becoming familiar with everything about the song including how I felt about each word. And, as recommended, I stayed at home doing nothing but preparation work all day long before the night of the concert.

Then fifteen minutes before the concert, Jorge rushed in announcing he couldn't bring his piano; he'd use his guitar instead. But I'd never sung to one. Then, during the first part of the concert, the director, with no warning, changed the order of the program.

When it came time for our duet, I nevertheless maintained a state of tranquil awareness, gazing at an audience of several hundred youthful Mexicans, and at one familiar face, Roland's. My voice projected warmly; I smiled when appropriate and sang the right notes even when my fellow singer harmonized incorrectly three times. Although two people in our group might have been considered professionals, after the concert the director praised only our song.

I didn't know I could learn to control myself so well. This is really amazing. What else can I do? Where else can I apply it? What would happen if everyone in the world applied training disciplines to their lives?

I tried to use some of the calming techniques in other fearful situations like being in groups or just to get to sleep at night. The intensity wore off when I didn't maintain a high level of practice, although the palm tree island image helped me for a couple of years.

Before we returned to Maine, Sareda gave me her bad news; her dermatologist had discovered a very ugly melanoma on her arm. I left for Kennebunk on a sad note.

ଔ

When I saw my relatives that summer in 2000, they spoke fondly about Conrad's wedding of the previous year, talking as though there had never been a rift between us.

I don't understand what's going on, but this may be the time for me to get over it. I've carried the grudge for almost twenty years! Take advantage of their talking with me. But be wiser now. No more taking things for granted with them—like believing that since they're cousins they should behave in a certain way, should care for me. I'll forget what happened after the fire. I know what I'll do: I'll pretend I don't know them at all and when we talk, it'll be as if I'm with someone I just met. If I like them, then fine, if not, so be it.

As a result, three cousins and I became better friends.

ଔ

After reading about Generation X in the *Atlantic Monthly*, Roland suggested we have an exhibition of their art, in all mediums including short film and digital images. The idea appealed to everyone on our Advisory Board, and we debated at length over the details for the call-for-work. We named the show, "The Unknown Generation X: Who Are We?" Hundreds of artists between the ages of eighteen and thirty-five responded from around the country. Our Advisory Board juried.

I'd always wanted to write about our exhibitions, but until now I'd never taken time out of my hectic schedule to do it. But after writing an arts column in San Miguel, I was more in tune to do it, and I interviewed a dozen Generation X'ers who worked in an upscale advertising and marketing firm housed in the same building as the gallery. This enabled me to include their ideas, fears and hopes in a lengthy article as part of the press release.

The newspapers liked it–it stimulated dialogue–and for the first time, almost all the newspapers in central Maine devoted one or two full pages in anticipation of one of our exhibitions. We put the article on our website together with the images from the show.

Having written the story, this exhibition was different for me. I felt personal satisfaction, as if I'd provided something special, because this time I used more than managerial skills. I used creative talent.

One afternoon after the opening, I was reviewing a call-for-work with Mike, the head of the art department at the University of Southern Maine and a member of our Advisory Board. Mike created large site-specific sculpture from hay; one year he filled the Great Hall at the Portland Museum of Art with hay boats suspended from the ceiling.

Halfway through our work, he stopped and looked at me. "I liked your article." I saw appreciation in his eyes and then slowly, all over his face. His compliment produced my first joyful, warm head-to-toe feeling. ***I'm experiencing the feeling of bliss, the heart-tugging, warm emotion I see on artists' faces when someone compliments their work at openings. Now I know what I want to do. Write. I've discovered my passion!***

As I prepared to leave for Mexico, a bit of my new halo, a product from uncovering my creative talent went into my suitcase. Roland and I also packed wedding clothes; Anthony and Joy's marriage would take place in London on January 27, 2001. We were flying there from Mexico City.

ʚ

From the start, Joy's parents made us feel welcome. Mr. Patel extended an open invitation. "Helen and Roland, you must come to stay with us when you get tired of living in Anthony and Joy's house in Essex. Here you'll be closer to downtown. Our place is simple, but you're welcome to stay for as long as you like."

Anthony had told me that some important people from India, including a Chief Justice of the Supreme Court, stayed with his in-laws. I knew they had money: they'd given Joy and Anthony a generous down payment for a house and a brand-new red Toyota. I wondered what their home would be like.

We walked up a long flight of narrow stairs covered with sky blue, commercial-quality carpet into an apartment built in the Victorian era. The blue carpet was present everywhere, including the third floor, which we had to ourselves. Thick, yellowy-white paint covered the walls. The only furnishings in the living room consisted of the same carpet, family photos, inexpensive pictures of Hindu deities, a plain brown leather couch without cushions, three matching armchairs and a television.

After welcoming us, Mrs. Patel gave us tea and cookies. Shortly, Joy's father brought out crackers, cheese and vintage malt Scotch whisky, although neither he nor Mrs. Patel drink. After enjoying the Scotch and conversation, we sat in the dining room at a white wooden table with a checkered yellow and white vinyl cloth to eat about ten dishes of succulent vegetarian foods, all prepared by our hostess, all from carefully selected ingredients found at the Indian marketplace. It was hard to stop eating, especially the two speckled yellow breads I'd not previously seen or tasted.

Flying home over the Atlantic snuggled against Roland, I made a conscious decision not to worry about Anthony being so far away. *The Patels are different—they practice the Hindu spirit of generosity. Anthony sensed my initial uneasiness and told me not to worry, that wherever he was, he'd always love me. What a loving, kind and unique person. I'm so blessed to have him for a son. He was on his own all those years in Venezuela. I have faith he won't be swallowed up and removed from my life by his in-laws who look and speak differently. It feels strange but good and warm to have faith and trust in my son, in his new family and to allow these feelings to override my fear of losing him. I feel so good about him and me—as if I'm maturing.*

16

In the Middle

I began studying Lenore Thomson's book ***Personality Type: An Owner's Manual*** a little over a year after I'd glanced through it. Foremost, I learned two things: half the world shared introversion with me, and being in my inner world as an introvert was normal, not strange, just different from extroverts. I underlined passages, made comments in the margins and wrote questions on the blank sheets in the back, such as, "Do introverts stay in the background all the time while extroverts make themselves heard?"

After reading the chapters on introversion and extroversion, I began the ones on Jungian typology. This section intrigued me more. Jung's types were so well depicted, so real life. I could see parts of his human personality types all around me: Roland as the thinker introvert, Sareda as a feeling extrovert. I couldn't figure out which of Jung's eight basic types I was, but unlike my hesitation with discovering my personality type in the ancient Chinese Enneagram, now I was determined to learn my type and utilize it for self-growth.

For by this time I realized that I'd been ignored for much of my life because my inward-looking personality wasn't very available to others. Ironically, I'd failed to care for myself by being overwhelmed by shyness and its ramifications.

Ignited by Thomson's book and fueled by the presence of friends and my fledgling confidence, I decided the next topic I wanted to write about was how introversion affected my childhood and how it closeted my personality for just about all my life. I would write it the best way I knew how, from the heart, like I did for my talk, "Unitarianism from the Heart."

When I saw an article in the San Miguel newspaper about Jungian Archetypal Drama Workshops, I signed up right away, hoping it would broaden my knowledge of Jungian theory.

On the day of the first workshop, not wanting to arrive early and have to talk with people, and not wanting to arrive late and miss something, I got there exactly on time. The leader, Bill, came straight over to greet me, his loose-fitting sandals barely able to keep up with him. In his late fifties, he wore baggy jeans and a loose fitting shirt that hung over his protruded belly. His encouraging voice allayed some of my fears which the word ***drama*** had aroused.

Only three others were there, chatting with one another in front of the coffeepot. I didn't want to join them, but now at least I understood why and felt all right about it: our behavior merely reflected that of extroverts and introverts.

As soon as we sat, I became more at ease, even though by now I knew I was in for a healing workshop rather than lectures about Jung. In order to center us, Bill read us a poem and after describing "archetypal" as universal qualities such as trust, love, and envy, he said each of us would have a chance to work out a problem using drama.

In the third workshop, I volunteered to dramatize one. I chose to sit on the floor, legs bent under me, and leaning over on top of my thighs, with my head down, I hugged my knees, pulling myself into the smallest possible pose. Already crying, I began, "My emotions are hardened, locked, as if twisted in a huge knot. It stays in my stomach." I continued to cry—and cried throughout. "I hated my childhood. I was locked up in my room much of the time."

Soon we did role-playing in which others asked me questions from the point of view of each of my parents and in turn I spoke from my parents' points of view as well as from my own. After about thirty minutes, Bill provided suggestions to "close" my wound. Then he asked me to say how the experience affected me, and the others said what my story meant to them.

I was opening my cache of emotional pain, by far the hardest endeavor of my life. The experience was as monumental and wonderful as a cripple learning to throw away crutches. It immediately gave me a degree self-respect, self-confidence and self-composure, and I knew more would come. As a result of continued talk and writing about the buried pain, over a few years and with more professional help, most old hurts vanished. I can now identify others who haven't yet faced their old pain by telltale signs, such as not behaving freely and openly.

At home the day after revealing my soul in Bill's group, I reflected on my bravery, my actions. *Were the others shocked? Will they think I'm strange, an oddball for storing all those hurts all these years... I did what I had to. I feel stronger for having done it and I can't worry about them.* We flew into Boston during a freak April snowstorm, and, for the second year in a row, had to drive to Portland. This time, though, I didn't let my emotions bother me while we passed through Kennebunk. I was learning not to upset myself, to practice the art of controlling my consciousness, as advised in the book Kathleen had recommended, *Flow,* by M. Csikszentmihalyi.

ᴓ

The arts editor for the *Portland Press Herald* visited Roland and me and explained why her paper didn't cover our exhibitions more often. "Alternative galleries aren't sexy; there's no glamour." I pictured the Portland Museum of Art and its Winslow Homer and other famous collections, lavish openings and black-tie dinners enticing the wealthy, whose presence in turn draws middle-class art lovers who provide additional support.

I'd struggled to raise money and grow our gallery for twelve exciting years. I loved its exhibitions, artists, volunteers and Advisory Board. However, despite Roland's protests, after a long period of inner reflection and consideration of my priorities, I resigned. I hoped someone would volunteer to be the director for personal reasons, for love of art or to help them grow as the gallery helped me, but it was impossible to find that person. No one else would take my place because the gallery couldn't offer a salary. We closed the gallery after a drawing exhibition called "From New York to Newfoundland."

Danforth Gallery, the Maine Artists Space had done well: it lasted considerably longer than most alternative galleries. I now believe my initial ignorance of the art world, my inability to understand our mission statement and my introverted and shy personality hindered my chances to raise more money. However, for many years, several hundred of us did our best to put on some of the best exhibitions of the times in Maine, and a few years later, it pleased me to hear that Danforth Gallery was sorely missed.

For a week we sorted out stuff, throwing away most of it, putting up salable articles in a yard sale. It seemed as if the gallery disappeared overnight. For a few years Roland kept some of the work exhibited online, but I wanted nothing more to do with it.

For, by this time, in 2001, at age fifty-nine, I felt equipped to be me and I knew what I wanted to do. I wanted to write and I knew my subject.

ᘓ

During the last exhibition in July, I started reading Jung's *Psychological Types.* It horrified me to read some of the ideas people held about introverts. Jung, an introvert himself, wrote some of the most condemning theories. I'm including a few paragraphs to illustrate not only the harsh description but also what I went through in struggling to understand him.

> [The introvert] is apt to appear awkward, often seeming inhibited, and it frequently happens that, by a certain brusqueness of manner, or by his glum inapproachability, or some kind of malapropism, he causes unwitting offense to people. He suspects all kinds of bad motives, has an everlasting fear of making a fool of himself, is usually very touchy and surrounds himself with a barbed

> wire entanglement so dense and impenetrable that finally he himself would rather do anything but sit behind it.

I read his descriptions of introverted types several times and made notes if I needed ideas clarified. I started a notebook about characteristics of extroverts and introverts. I thought about people who were instrumental in my life, such as my parents and about their degrees of these two traits. From this, I began writing a chronology of my life and how introversion affected me at different ages.

Now I wanted to learn my type and also get help in understanding several of Jung's concepts. It didn't occur to me to see a Jungian analyst; I had a vague notion they were stuffy specialists who counseled the same esoteric, wealthy clientele for years.

I don't know how Jung would describe what happened next.

The very day I left Danforth Gallery for good, the day of the yard sale, as I exited the main door to the street, I glanced to the right and saw a stack of free Portland newspapers. For over a dozen years I'd struggled to entice its art reviewers to cover our shows and so, upon seeing the paper, I sighed in relief knowing I didn't need to read it anymore. But then I reconsidered. Well, why not read it for myself, for me, and picked one up.

That evening, sitting alone at our dining-room table in the Pool House, half listening to geese overhead, I noticed the photo on the paper's cover: the Jung Center in Brunswick. Within a three-page article, I learned that its president, Chris Beach, worked in Portland and for a nominal fee would determine a person's type. I left a message on his answering machine, which he soon returned.

"It'll take a few sessions to learn your type, Helen, but I can see you this Friday at two and we'll get started. I'm on Pleasant Street. Do you know where that is?"

I could hardly speak. "Yes, I know where it is. See you Friday." *His office was right beside Danforth Gallery! These coincidences are too much. What can they mean? I don't really believe in them, yet I do—Bill's workshop, Sareda's extroversion, my Flow and Shyness books, finding the newspaper article the day I left the gallery and Chris's office being right next to where I've lived and worked for twelve years. It's not like following my bliss, but it's akin to it. I think it means I'm doing what I should be doing.*

ଔ

Chris met me in the communal waiting room. Dressed in Bermuda shorts, sandals and a long-sleeved white sweatshirt, he smiled broadly when he shook my hand, saying he was pleased to meet me, in an accent that wasn't from Maine. He told me he'd had two prior careers, teacher and lawyer. His homey office with simple furniture felt comfortable.

For two sessions, I filled out a standard questionnaire on psychological types and responded to questions Chris asked. Afterward he said I was an INFJ, which stands for introverted, intuitive, feeling and judging. While he told me a few salient characteristics of my type, I took notes and the following is compiled from them.

Some studies suggest that only 1 to 2 percent of the total population is INFJ, so it's hard for us to find people similar to ourselves, especially playmates in the early years. My type has difficulty getting close to our feelings. We tend to think that others understand us even when we don't explain anything. We dislike having to ask for help. We can be stubborn.

You mean there are others like me? I'm supposed to be this way? I'm not off balance...I'm just being me? Wow. If only I'd been taught about differences in personalities as a child, I wouldn't have suffered during all those years. I could have learned to enjoy people. I needed to know I was normal. I hope today's parents will learn about this and help their shy children.

I didn't mention anything to Chris during my initial interviews about my personal problems, but after he explained my type, I told him I was studying Jung to learn about introverts and extroverts. I said I needed help to understand Jung and asked Chris if he would help me if I compiled a list of questions. He said he would and agreed to be my mentor. I went home and read Jung's description of my type several times, feeling excited while trying to make sense of it.

Jung writes that INFJ's are the hardest type for anyone to get to know. I understood him to say that in the depth of our psychic world, our unconscious can fathom all of the images that ever existed in the human race. Most visionaries, he says, are INFJ's and without us there would have been no prophets in Israel.

We introverts do stay on the quiet side, but we're important to the world! We give it shape! Without us, extroverts wouldn't know how to run it. It's so comforting to know we serve such a valuable role, even if it's not much noticed.

I knew but didn't care that the Jungian belief system wasn't totally accurate, that it wasn't an exact science. Jung himself said that when people learned more about human character someone would supplant his typology system with another. To my knowledge, although several people have tried to do so, many corporations still use the Myer and Briggs adaptation of Jungian typology for hiring and human resource issues.

In studying my type, one thing in particular intrigued me: the nature of the secondary function. Mine was called extroverted feeling, and I couldn't understand how anything labeled extrovert could apply to me. Chris explained, "The primary way you relate to the world is introverted, but, you have a secondary way—one almost as strong as the primary one—called extroverted feeling. This means you have the ability within you, a built-in talent you were born with, to connect to and relate with the outside world."

When the definition sank in, I felt a tremendous surge. It was like telling a person with half-closed eyes, "If you open them more, you can see better."

Roland and I hadn't gone to church for years because the gallery had taken up all our energy, and with the gallery closed, contact with people lessened. But I wanted to try out my extroverted feeling trait so much that I was willing to do it anywhere, for example, with people at a store or in the library.

I spoke as if it were natural for me to mention the obvious; for example, looking at a stranger with a smile and enthusiasm, I would say, "Did you see the fog this morning?" The person would smile at me and add a pleasantry. Then soon to my astonishment I realized getting warm responses was even easier than that. I didn't need to say anything at all. Just giving a simple, warm smile to someone usually caused them to smile back. ***My goodness, it's so easy! I'll never be tongue-tied again! Instead of drawing away from people, I look forward to them!***

In addition to reading Jung and Thomson about extroverts and introverts, I decided to expand my knowledge on this subject the best way I knew how, doing interviews. I'd learned so much doing them when I prepared talks for the Unitarian Fellowship and for my art column. The process gave me a position of authority, of leadership, but more important, during the interviews I became an inquisitive person interested in the world and people. This was my true nature, of course, but normally, being shy, I had no way to show it. I spent several days developing ideas to use in a questionnaire.

When Roland and I flew to San Miguel in 2001, I guarded my project in a carry-on so it wouldn't get lost. Captive to the drone of big jets, I contemplated Chris's fee schedule: "Eighty dollars an hour or whatever you can afford–you decide." I couldn't believe his willingness or sincerity to help people. It felt good to know if I lacked money, I could still consult him.

☙

Once in San Miguel I couldn't wait to finish the questionnaire. Here is part of the introduction and some questions, as I wrote them then:

> Chaucer wrote, "My mind to me a kingdom is; such present joys therein I find, that it excels all other bliss that earth affords." Historically, introverts have been frequently misunderstood in a negative fashion. The goal of my research is to underscore positive characteristics of introverts. This is a project I am designing and undertaking that will collect

descriptions from people about introvert and extrovert characteristics. The project will focus on ideas, relationships and activities in and of themselves and in the context, among other things, of religion, race, age, education, upbringing, parenting, crime, and government policies.

Introverts look inward for meaning to life, for energy, for inspiration, and extroverts look to the exterior world for motivation, purpose and energy. Both types are natural; one seeks to provide spiritual peace for inner realms, and the other seeks to give direction and cohesiveness to the outer world. We all have aspects of both, but one comes more predominantly to us than the other.

In our meetings, I shall ask you to describe in detail some relationships where you especially notice the presence or absence of introvert and extrovert influences. Names of interviewees will not be released. I'll be writing down your answers.

When did you first become aware of extrovert/introvert behavior?

What was it like for you as a child in your family? Were your needs met? What about later, as a teenager, both with your family and with friends?

Talk about your values, passions, what you do about them and how they mesh with your introversion or extroversion.

What would you recommend to our educational system or society to provide more awareness of introversion and extroversion?

> How can introverts be made to feel more important, for example, in initiation ceremonies that are geared for extroverts, when bullies and talkers get all the attention?

I interviewed thirty people in San Miguel for at least ninety minutes each, without straying from my list of questions. I began with two people from the bridge club and asked each one for names of others. I advertised in the newspaper and three people responded. I interviewed Unitarians, artists and acquaintances, such as Bill from the therapy workshop and his girlfriend. There were more women than men, and many respondents were sixty or over. We met at cafés, unless I knew them well enough to go to their homes. I didn't use anything a professional interviewer might have used except for my questionnaire.

People responded with interest and sincerity. Most were introverts and were keen about the idea of making the world a better place for them. Like I, many felt left out at parties and in group meetings and their descriptions of feelings of isolation magnified my interest in my project. They also helped me feel less alone in my sometimes, involuntary solitary world.

Three of the interviewees became friends. One, Ping, especially liked what I was doing. "Why don't you come visit me in Canada, and you can interview all my friends. Come for August tenth; I'll be having a party to celebrate the opening of the Buddhist prayer hut I'm building beside my pond. You can speak with my guests and arrange a time to interview them."

"That sounds very interesting. Thank you. I'll call you about it when I get to Maine."

ଔ

At the same time I did the interviews, I continued to write about my life. I told Sareda that I was writing about some of the problems I suffered while growing up, and she invited me to join her writers' group. I was nervous to be part of a group, a writers' one at that, and especially queasy about sharing my story, but I knew it would be a good learning step. I asked her to read my work for me, because I feared I'd break down. But when she missed a session, I had to read it myself.

In order not to lose control, I tried to concentrate more on how I spoke and less on the content. In my interviews I'd listened to many people describe their sad childhoods, but I'd not spoken about mine and now it was hard. One day, someone in the group, herself a therapist, asked, "How can you be shy and still read this?"

I choked down my feelings, holding back tears. "It's not easy."

I started to realize just how much I'd missed out on in the world by not expressing myself and that hurt. I knew I had to educate myself not to despair in self-pity over my prior isolation.

So I pushed myself and didn't let anything prevent me from continuing in the group. But, there was another part to being a member of the writers' group: critiquing. How could I—I who knew next to nothing about writing—critique someone? But then a member read from her story about some rowdy cowboys on horseback shooting hens and I saw an opportunity derived from my childhood knowledge of hens on Prince Edward Island. "That wouldn't happen: you'd need a shotgun to hit a hen running around because they run so quickly, and cowboys carry rifles." She thanked me. Gradually, I began commenting on style. I felt so accomplished and happy to be a member of a writers' group.

Toward the end of that winter I gave Sareda my life story to edit. Then it consisted of thirty pages. "It's way too long, Helen. You have to shorten it a lot."

I made some changes per her edits and, wanting more feedback, asked Bill from the Jungian Drama Workshop if he would read it. It was hot out, so we sat outdoors under a row of sculpted trees in the town square as he read it. When he finished, he put it down and rubbed the back of his neck awhile before he spoke. "This is pretty heavy stuff. I don't know what to say, but I know what you mean, though, since I was shy in high school, especially at the dances."

I felt horrified that he would compare what I underwent with an occasional shy feeling in high school. But, right there and then, on that hot day in the center of San Miguel, it became apparent that if Bill, himself a therapist, didn't understand how I experienced shyness, then something was very amiss. I decided to show my story to Chris, along with the interviews he'd agreed to look at, when I returned to Maine the following month.

Roland didn't go back to Kennebunk with me. He stayed on in Mexico an additional two months to paint. Now that he didn't have a workplace at Danforth Gallery and our home in Kennebunk had none, he was without a studio. Over time he grew more and more dissatisfied, and by 2006 our relationship deteriorated to the extent I had to leave him. I felt as if he were strangling me, and since he wouldn't see a counselor, I had no alternative but to live alone. I felt very brave to go out on my own, but I did. Afterward, we both suffered enormously, but that part of my life is not relevant here. However, I'll add that his behavior changed so radically that after almost three years we are now able to enjoy living together again, at least for some of the year.

ଔ

I mailed Chris my story and interviews and met with him on a warm day at the end of May 2002. He began the session, "For me it would be hard to write a book about introverts and extroverts, and I have some background. I don't see how you're going to be able to do it." After he let that sink in, he continued, "Helen, I read your story. What you went through as a child wasn't because you're an introvert. Being locked up, not having children to play with at home—you went through major family obstacles—I'd call it abuse."

Trembling with an unknown feeling and on the verge of tears, I asked, "You would? How would you rank it?"

"Extreme. Being locked up and having no one to play with added to your shy nature, making it acute. But, it had little to do with being an introvert. Not all introverts are shy. You didn't feel bad because you were an introvert, but because you suffered from being shut up and having no friends."

"I was so shy all of my life," I cried, sobbing, gulping for air. I could go no further.

"I understand your pain. There's a terrible, enormous bias against shyness in this country; it's held by everyone, and that includes us psychologists."

On my drive home, I wiped off streams of tears so I could see. *I can't write about extroverts and introverts; I'm not professional in that, as Chris says. Besides, it would be too factual and not much about me. I want to write from the heart, because that comes naturally and I know people like it. So I have to write about me...write about my shyness. Can I be so brave?*

In the days that followed, partly from excitement and partly from fright, I could think of little else. My goal was clear, though. I wanted to encourage shy people to get professional help by using my experience as an example. And, I wanted to write my story in such a way it would clarify the nature of severe shyness so the non-shy could understand us better. I decided to add some direct references to shyness in my questionnaire to learn what others thought about it. The following was a new question:

> Shyness is often confused with introversion. Introverts, how do you feel about that? How many times is it that you refrain from speaking because you wish to be quiet, or do you refrain because of shyness? As an extrovert, are you shy sometimes? Describe a time you felt shy and how it makes you feel.

With the new questionnaire, I interviewed five acquaintances in Kennebunk, and through my friend Greta, the yoga teacher whom I'd met in San Miguel, half a dozen people in Lexington, Massachusetts.

Several ideas and events unfolded to further help me. Chris suggested I do workshops in adult education on overcoming shyness. I liked the idea and started making an outline for it. It helped me focus my approach to explaining shyness to put myself in the shoes of other shy people and to consider how to approach them. I would conduct the workshop in San Miguel. To learn some writing skills, I signed up for a writers' workshop at Haystack, the artists' retreat on Deer Isle near Blue Hill, where my father's family had summered.

Then, for a couple of days, I visited my friend Diane on Long Island where she and her husband now lived. At an outdoor café, I read her a few pages, crying nonstop.

"Helen, this is so wonderful! You'll be writing a memoir, and you and your children will feel so good about it. I really admire you."

I wanted to say, "I'm writing it more for shy people," but I was too bashful.

Next I called Ping. "Is the invitation to visit with you still open?" Soon I was flying up Vermont Interstate 91 en route to Hadley, a tiny village in the rolling mountains of the Eastern Townships, just over the Canadian border.

Seek and you shall find: now I know to seek with my heart and find with my heart, not with my eyes. Give and you shall receive—I give with my heart and receive with my heart, not with my mind. I have many, many more concepts to reconsider, but now I've started. My epiphany of so many years ago is paying off in spades. In many ways my life is just beginning.

I followed Ping's directions through Hadley's narrow roads to her house. The next day, a beautiful one, while her guests celebrated the Buddhist prayer house, I spoke with twelve people, making appointments with each one. I wasn't shy for a minute. On the contrary, I started to look forward to meeting people, eager to hear what they had to say, instead of looking at people as potential instruments of anxiety.

Back in Kennebunk, warm feelings flooded through my body in ways that were more profound, energizing and rewarding than anything I could have imagined years ago. *I'm understanding people! What's more, I'm relating to them! I can see everyone's wants, fears and needs as well as my own. It's so surprising, it's as if people are the same everywhere. I don't for a moment take these good feelings for granted. I struggled long and hard for this and I'm going to stay on top of it.*

ଋ

It was soon after this, in 2002, that I stopped feeling bored or lonely. With my new interests, my level of self-consciousness probably continued to lessen, although I didn't think about that much anymore. By 2007 I felt even better. In Mexico I had half a dozen friends and attended writers' groups, the Duplicate Bridge Club, a singing group and a Philosophy discussion group.

I sometimes had significant personal moments. For example, in April 2008 during the period I spent six weeks at the Vermont Studio Center, a residency for writers, I dreamed a life-size white tiger came onto a busy university campus, singled me out and nuzzled my face with his for a few moments before trotting off. It made me feel I could do any worthwhile thing I chose and that I had a white tiger to protect me.

ଋ

In December 2008, I awoke with a strange feeling. It was as if a component in my brain had disappeared and I realized that shyness wasn't affecting me *at all.*

Nonetheless, a not unfamiliar pain, though one that's lost much of its punch, surfaces on occasion to remind me of past hurts. Sometimes it makes me weep and I remember that an instructor at Stonecoast Writers' Conference had said to me, "The pain's there; it's part of your humanity."

Last September my brother Nat visited Crescent Surf and stayed with me for a month. It was the first time I'd seen him without one of us having children or a spouse present and we were able to get to know each other for the first time. In Cos Cob and Prince Edward Island we'd led separate lives and in Portugal he was too busy with his young family and business to have time alone with me. It was gratifying to talk about things we shared in the past, especially about our parents.

During the last two or three years, I've meditated about my parents so much that now I can finally understand them better, and I'm comfortable with what I know about them as people. I treasure my mother's advice, "Count your blessings," and I try to live up to my father's favorite refrain, "Be yourself." I try to have one social activity a day and keep my life interesting at home when I'm alone by reading, writing or listening to music. When I feel I'm slipping into some kind of depression, and I do sometimes, I respond immediately and "fix" the problem myself or, if I can't, I consult with Chris.

Chris suggested some pastimes to help soothe my personality type, such as gardening and drawing. Although these two activities used to repulse me because they seemed so strange, when I draw I feel worn out and relaxed after about thirty minutes of making little designs with colored pencils and pens. So to get better when I'm feeling down, I draw, reflect on what's bothering me and count my blessings.

Chris gave me more advice, another exercise to feel centered and focused. For it, I write down some ideas I've been working on and go outdoors. There, sitting alone in a quiet frame of mind surrounded by nature, helpful thoughts come to me as if they were from another source. I write everything down. It's an intense time and doesn't last more than half an hour. This year, 2009, I began my study of Transcendentalism at the Friday Philosophy Discussion Group in San Miguel, and I believe my going outdoors to work on a problem may be kindred to what Thoreau and Emerson refer to when they speak of seeking inspiration from nature.

I keep my swimming pool blue and pretty-looking mainly because it symbolizes my drive to grow, mature and be free of shyness. Anthony and Joy use it during their visits from London and Conrad and Ellen when they're weekending here from Massachusetts. I love to watch their children, my grandchildren, Noah four and Simon two, experience the delightful thrill and scary unknown of having water under them, beside them and all around them, as their parents encourage them.

I had fewer friends in Kennebunk than in Mexico so recently I set a goal of making four new ones. I succeeded! This summer I am planning a swim party in my pool, like the one I gave last year with the new friends and two old ones. Last year's party was a glorious time for all. I was a little conscious of my childhood, of my journey to overcome shyness, but mainly I was in the moment, the greatest part of it all. I was in the middle of everything–splashing, talking and just plain enjoying.

Afterword

From: Debbie Burns
To: Helen R. Merrill
Sent: Thu, December 10, 2009 7:43:59 PM
Subject: YOU

Thinking of you.
Hope things are going well.

I expect being with the boys is a great uplift for you. Let me know how things are going when you have a chance.

Love, Debbie

Re: YOU
From: Helen Rivas-Rose
To: Debbie Burns
Sent: Sat, December 12, 2009 9:10:17 AM

Hi Debbie,

I made a significant discovery the other day while reading *Anti Cancer: A New Way of Life* by David Servan-Scheiber. He says old pain that lingers on with one from the past is not real; it is "false," an "illusion." My level of pain awareness ebbed almost immediately. It will be interesting to see how it plays out.

I can't help but think there's some connection between finishing my book and being diagnosed with cancer twenty-two days later.

My spirits are not bad. Dr. Erban from MGH said the single most important thing I can do is exercise and Dr. Miller, my neurosurgeon who helps me with my back, said it's imperative I walk every day until I break out in a light sweat because it releases endorphins that spread through my whole body. They help fight the cancer and help my system deal with the blow of learning I have cancer.

As I walk at my best speed through the snowy, cold and hilly neighborhood, I think of you and the fast, fast walk you used to do on the Boulevard.

Conrad and family left for a night yesterday and I missed them all, especially at suppertime. I am so blessed to be able to spend these six months with them.

Christmas is upon us all. The effects of my chemo have been light so far and I am hoping to consume a fair portion of Christmas dinner.

Wishing you well,
Love,
Helen

Acknowledgments

Little by little, over the last fifteen years, I've learned the world is full of kind, caring people.

With their support, I wrote nine hundred soulful pages, a personal account of how shyness has affected me.

My first professional editorial help came from Alan Rinzler of Jossey Bass. I rewrote the whole manuscript under his guidance. A fine and exacting editor, he helped me write considerably more coherently.

Several friends in various writers' groups offered help that was invaluable. My thanks to Sassy Smallman, author and Professor of English, who stuck by me always and, when I had no one else, edited several chapters, sometimes the same one more than once. Pauline Clift, gifted short story writer and a stickler for detail, had me read chapter 6 of John Gardner's book with its dire warnings about unsettling the poor reader with a wrongly chosen word. Oliver Payne, a consummate wordsmith, opened my eyes to a clearer sense of diction and presentation, and Cynthia Graves, author and English teacher, helped me clarify some of my personal viewpoints.

Bill Pearlman, a friend, therapist and author, offered several suggestions about both wording and content; my cousin John Bates helped with material on our family; and my brother Nat graciously read the material several times, offering his recollections.

Often the line between writers and friends blurs, but here's thanks to those I knew more as friends than writers: Diane Giardi, Lenore Weinstein, Lydia Cornwall Bishop, Carol Coolen, Jane Kent Rockwell, Elizabeth Hutz, Jean Dorr, and Mary Ann Brooks-Mueller. To those whom I've forgotten to mention, please accept my apologies.

Following Alan Rinzler, other editors helped along the way: Laura Josephs, Pat Walsh, and Cheri Long, each with caring and professional advice.

In the last stage, Erin Clermont edited the whole manuscript with an especially keen eye and sharp insight. With her help, I knew the writing was done.

Last, but most important, my gratitude to my wonderful children, Anthony and Conrad, who read many, many drafts and waited, patiently and lovingly, not knowing what would evolve.

About the Author

HELEN RIVAS-ROSE divides her time between two countries and two picturesque towns: Kennebunk, Maine, and San Miguel de Allende, Mexico. In both places she cultivates family, friendships and social activities, while always finding time to pursue her hard-won passion, writing. In both the States and Mexico she attends writing seminars, workshops and residencies and belongs to writers' groups. Developing her own artistic endeavors became essential to overcoming her shyness, and together with her social interests, constantly feed her vital interest in life.

Breinigsville, PA USA
21 June 2010

240314BV00001B/1/P